Brian Fitzgerald · Audris Mockus ·
Minghui Zhou

Editors

Towards Engineering Free/Libre Open Source Software (FLOSS) Ecosystems for Impact and Sustainability

Communications of NII Shonan Meetings

 Springer

Editors
Brian Fitzgerald
University of Limerick
Limerick, Ireland

Audris Mockus
University of Tennessee at Knoxville
Knoxville, USA

Minghui Zhou
Peking University
Beijing, China

ISBN 978-981-13-7101-1   ISBN 978-981-13-7099-1   (eBook)
https://doi.org/10.1007/978-981-13-7099-1

This Springer imprint is published by the registered company Springer Nature Singapore Pte Ltd.
The registered company address is: 152 Beach Road, #21-01/04 Gateway East, Singapore 189721, Singapore

Towards Engineering Free/Libre Open Source
Software (FLOSS) Ecosystems for Impact
and Sustainability

Preface

Free/libre open source (FLOSS) ecosystems such as the Linux kernel have had a tremendous impact on computing and society and have captured the attention of businesses, researchers, and policy-makers. Millions of participants, from independent volunteers to those representing companies or government organizations, have created and maintained massive numbers of software projects, ranging from individual scratch space or classroom assignments to critical infrastructure projects such as the Linux Kernel, OpenStack, Docker, or Android. The spectrum and scale of FLOSS has substantially expanded in recent years, as has its popularity. The combination of distributed version control and social media features has created "transparent" environments that facilitate the scaling up of the ecosystems to millions of repositories and developers [1]. Despite the substantial amount of research on FLOSS in disciplines such as software development, organizational science, management, and social science, it remains unclear how and why FLOSS ecosystems form, how they achieve their impact, or how they sustain themselves. The open nature of these communities and the associated vast collections of operational data represent a tantalizing possibility to discover the mechanisms by which such ecosystems form and operate. Achieving such understanding would inform approaches to structuring future open-source communities, and could reveal ways to nudge the behavior of individuals and groups involved toward greater sustainability of FLOSS ecosystems.

Research on FLOSS phenomena has been ongoing for almost two decades. From an economic perspective, the most common topics involve motivation and organization: Why do the participants in FLOSS contribute without material compensation usually, and how do such apparently unstructured and distributed organizations survive and succeed? Early research focused on understanding the nature of FLOSS development practice and the reasons underpinning FLOSS success [2, 3], the study of user innovation [4, 5], and the motivation of participants [6, 7]. A great deal of effort has been devoted to investigating communities, e.g., the strategies and processes by which newcomers join [8].

The nature of group and ecosystem sustainability has also been investigated. For example, how a sustainable group evolves [9], how online communities should encourage commitment [10], how successful FLOSS project participants progressively enroll a network of human and material allies to support their efforts [11], how the congruence of values between the individual and their organization affects turnover [12], and what impact the initial willingness and project environment have on newcomers' long-term participation [13, 14].

As commercial participation in FLOSS has become common, the question of how to combine FLOSS practice with commercial practice has received more attention. For example, how the new phenomenon (OSS 2.0) is significantly different from its FLOSS antecedent is discussed in [15]. Borrowing FLOSS style project structure, many organizations are embracing a global sourcing strategy which has been termed open sourcing [16]. Successful hybrid projects have been studied to help understand how to improve upon existing software development practice. The motivation of commercial participation has also been extensively studied, see, e.g., [17, 18, 19, 20]. Various business strategies have been identified and analyzed in, e.g., [21, 22, 23, 24]. The impact that commercial participation has on communities is also being studied currently [25, 26]. The FLOSS phenomenon has also served as a proof-of-concept which has led to interest in initiatives such as inner source [27] and crowdsourcing [28, 29].

The importance of FLOSS ecosystems, and the general lack of understanding on how they function, was the impetus for our Shonan meeting in June of 2017. The specific questions prominent researchers were asked to discuss include the following:

1. How does an ecosystem form? How do different stakeholders work together to form a community that develops and maintains valuable and freely available software, and how does an ecosystem with millions of repositories and developers operate given the lack of centralized planning?
2. How is the ecosystem organized? How do the teams cooperate to resolve the issues (workflow), and what are the typical relationships between the code and the team?
3. How does the ecosystem evolve in response to the environment as technology and needs evolve over time?
4. What distinguishes ecosystems that sustain themselves from ecosystems that disappear? How can an ecosystem be sustained? Under what circumstances should it be sustained?
5. How do newcomers learn the protocols and practices of an ecosystem? How would they sustain the ecosystem? What is the relationship between people sustainability and ecosystem sustainability?
6. What kinds of research methods might be utilized (e.g., which qualitative and quantitative methods) to achieve research goals?

The results of the meeting are presented in the remaining chapters of this book. As FLOSS is a complex phenomenon, we first need to develop ways to measure it. Being able to measure relevant aspects of the ecosystem is critical to being able to quantify and understand how it operates.

> *"When you can measure what you are speaking about, and express it in numbers, you know something about it; but when you cannot measure it, when you cannot express it in numbers, your knowledge is of a meager and unsatisfactory kind."*—Lord Kelvin

To that extent, a critical role is played by networks of code flow, knowledge flow, and the technical dependencies. Measurement is further complicated by the volume, complexity, low quality, and rapidly changing data. The chapters in this book outline the general strategies of addressing some of these major challenges.

Once the measurement framework is established, we can build and, based on empirical measurements, falsify theories of FLOSS ecosystem. Perhaps, the most fundamental aspect of such ecosystems is related to software production: why developers contribute their code and are others willing to appropriate it? Early work on open source suggested that developers produce code for their own use, and hence sharing it is an incidental no-cost activity. Production in the present capitalist economy is, on the other hand, of dual purpose with more focus on the exchange value of goods.

> *"For two-fold is the use of every object.... The one is peculiar to the object as such, the other is not, as a sandal which may be worn, and is also exchangeable. Both are uses of the sandal, for even he who exchanges the sandal for the money or food he is in want of, makes use of the sandal as a sandal. But not in its natural way. For it has not been made for the sake of being exchanged."*

This fundamental property of any object (including software) suggests that the purely noneconomic explanation is lacking in depth and exchange should be important aspect of software production in addition to its use value (for personal use). Most of the code is designed to do very specific things and is not replaceable by other code (unlike, for example, commodities such as grain or metal): how do developers establish its exchange value? *"Exchange,"* Aristotle says, *"cannot take place without equality, and equality not without commensurability.[1]"* The later research on open source argued that what is being "exchanged" is a reputation that brings with it the ability for the reputation owner to make decisions and to influence others. They also point out that the reputation ultimately results in material outcomes, such as employment. Since FLOSS is heavily supported by corporations, it would probably be naive, therefore, to think that producing use value is the primary (or even a significant) driver of FLOSS development effort. This suggests that the exchange value of FLOSS software can be quantified as the amount of labor invested in producing the aspects of software that are useful to others: in other words, it is a social construct by nature. It is, obviously, not the actual amount of time a specific developer has invested in it, but depends on the productivity of that developer and ability of others to implement similar functionality, but it still can be

---

[1] Aristotle,*"De Rep."* l. i. c. 9.

quantified by these uniform units of labor derived from the actual time spent and capabilities of the implementer. As such, more direct ways to monetize such labor are being deployed in practice, such as Patreon, which enables fans and sponsors to give ongoing support to creators, and License Zero which requires commercial users to pay for a commercial license after 90 days. Furthermore, facilitators of exchange of such labor to material goods are facilitated by platforms such as Tidelift, which touts itself as a market for FLOSS developers building a sustainable business around their projects, or Open Collective, which provides tools and mechanisms for "collectives" to receive and spend money in a democratic and transparent way. The chapter on ecosystem microeconomics proposes an approach to conduct research on this, apparently novel, form of production, while chapters on licensing discuss details of protecting the resulting intellectual capital.

To function and survive, ecosystems need to attract people, get them onboarded and retain them. This necessitates evolving mechanisms for adapting to internal and external changes that pose risks. The chapters on the lifeblood of FLOSS ecosystems discuss possibilities for attracting, onboarding, and retaining contributors (and users), and eventually the death of ecosystems.

In the final two chapters, a variety of problems ranging from practical questions of how the government might engage in support of FLOSS ecosystems to methodology and implementation of building FLOSS collaboration platform in China are discussed.

Limerick, Ireland
Knoxville, USA
Beijing, China

Brian Fitzgerald
Audris Mockus
Minghui Zhou

References

1. J. Herbsleb, C. Kstner, C. Bogart, Intelligently transparent software ecosystems. IEEE Softw. **33**(1), 89–96 (2016)
2. A. Mockus, R.F. Fielding, J. Herbsleb, A case study of open source development: the Apache server, in *22nd International Conference on Software Engineering*, Limerick, Ireland, 4–11 June 2000, pp. 263–272. [Online]. Available: http://dl.acm.org/authorize?2580
3. B. Fitzgerald, Has open source a future?, in *Perspectives on Free and Open Source Software*, eds. J. Feller, B. Fitzgerald, S. Hissam, K. Lakhani (MIT Press, Cambridge, 2005), pp. 121–140
4. E. von Hippel, G. von Krogh, Open source software and the private-collective innovation model: issues for organization science. Organ. Sci. **14**(2), 209–223 (2003)
5. B. Fitzgerald, Open source software implementation: anatomy of success and failure. Int. J. Open Source Softw. Processes **1**(1), 1–19 (2009)
6. G. von Krogh, S. Haefliger, S. Spaeth, M. Wallin, Open source software: what we know (and do not know) about motivations to contribute, in *DRUID Conference 2008*, the University of Gothenburg research seminar, and the Open and User Innovation Workshop 2008 at Harvard Business School (2008)

7. J.A. Roberts, I.-H. Hann, S.A. Slaughter, Understanding the motivations, participation, and performance of open source software developers: a longitudinal study of the apache projects. Manage. Sci. **52**(7), 984–999 (2006)
8. G. von Krogh, S. Spaeth, K.R. Lakhani, Community, joining, and specialization in open source software innovation: a case study. Res. Policy **32**(7), 1217–1241 (2003)
9. S. O'Mahony, F. Ferraro, The emergence of governance in an open source community. Acad. Manage. J. **50**(5), 1079–1106 (2007)
10. R.E. Kraut, P. Resnick, *Building Successful Online Communities: Evidence-Based Social Design* (MIT Press, Cambridge, MA, 2012)
11. N. Ducheneaut, Socialization in an open source software community: a socio-technical analysis. J. Comput. Support. Collaborative Work **32**, 323–368 (2005)
12. B.J. Hoffman, D.J. Woehr, A quantitative review of the relationship between person organization fit and behavioral outcomes. J. Vocat. Behav. **68**(3), 389–399 (2006). [Online]. Available: http://www.sciencedirect.com/science/article/pii/S000187910500103X
13. M. Zhou, A. Mockus, Does the initial environment impact the future of developers? in *ICSE 2011*, Honolulu, Hawaii, 21–28 May 2011, pp. 271–280. [Online]. Available: http://dl.acm.org/authorize?414944
14. M. Zhou, A. Mockus, Who will stay in the floss community? modeling participant's initial behavior. IEEE Trans. Softw. Eng. **41**(1), 82–99 (2015)
15. B. Fitzgerald, The transformation of open source software. MIS Q. **30**(3), 587–598 (2006)
16. P.J. Agerfalk, B. Fitzgerald, Outsourcing to an unknown workforce: exploring opensourcing as a global sourcing strategy. MIS Q. **32**(2), 385–409 (2008). [Online]. Available: http://dl.acm.org/citation.cfm?id=2017366.2017375
17. A. Bonaccorsi, C. Rossi, Comparing motivations of individual programmers and firms to take part in the open source movement: from community to business. Knowl. Technol. Policy **18**(4), 40–64 (2006)
18. K. Crowston, K. Wei, J. Howison, A. Wiggins, Free/libre open source software development: what we know and what we do not know. ACM Comput. Surv. **44**, 02/2012 (2012)
19. P. Capek, S. Frank, S. Gerdt, D. Shields, A history of IBM's open-source involvement and strategy. IBM Syst. J. **44**(2), 249–257 (2005)
20. J. Henkel, Selective revealing in open innovation processes: the case of embedded linux. Res. Policy **35**, 953–969 (2006)
21. A. Bonaccorsi, S. Giannangeli, C. Rossi, Entry strategies under competing standards: hybrid business models in the open source software industry. Manage. Sci. **52**(7), 1085–1098 (2006)
22. N. Munga, T. Fogwill, Q. Williams, The adoption of open source software in business models: a red hat and IBM case study, in *The 2009 Annual Research Conference of the South African Institute of Computer Scientists and Information Technologists*, October 2009
23. L. Dahlander, M. Magnusson, How do firms make use of open source communities? Long Range Plann. **41**(6), 629–649 (2008). [Online]. Available: http://www.sciencedirect.com/science/article/pii/S0024630108000836
24. P. Wagstrom, J. Herbsleb, R. Kraut, A. Mockus, The impact of commercial organizations on volunteer participation in an online community, in *Academy of Management Annual Meeting*, Montreal, CA, 6–10 August 2010
25. X. Ma, M. Zhou, D. Riehle, How commercial involvement affects open source projects: three case studies on issue reporting. Sci. China Inf. Sci. **56**(8), pp. 1–13 (2013)
26. M. Zhou, A. Mockus, X. Ma, L. Zhang, H. Mei, Inflow and retention in OSS communities with commercial involvement: a case study of three hybrids. ACM Trans. Softw. Eng. Methodol (TOSEM) (2016)
27. K. Stol, P. Avgeriou, M. Babar, Y. Lucas, B. Fitzgerald, Key factors for adopting inner source. ACM Trans. Softw. Eng. Methodol. **23**(2)

28. K. Stol, B. Fitzgerald, Twos company, threes a crowd: a case study of crowdsourcing software development, in *Proceedings of International Conference on Software Engineering*, 2014
29. K. Stol, B. Caglayan, B. Fitzgerald, Competition-based crowdsourcing software development: a multi-method study from a customer perspective. IEEE Trans. Softw. Eng. (2018). https://doi.org/10.1109/tse.2017.2774297

Contents

Chapter 1
A Methodology for Measuring FLOSS Ecosystems

Sadika Amreen, Bogdan Bichescu, Randy Bradley, Tapajit Dey,
Yuxing Ma, Audris Mockus, Sara Mousavi and Russell Zaretzki

Abstract FLOSS ecosystem as a whole is a critical component of world's computing infrastructure, yet not well understood. In order to understand it well, we need to
measure it first. We, therefore, aim to provide a framework for measuring key aspects
of the entire FLOSS ecosystem. We first consider the FLOSS ecosystem through lens
of a supply chain. The concept of supply chain is the existence of series of interconnected parties/affiliates each contributing unique elements and expertise so as
to ensure a final solution is accessible to all interested parties. This perspective has
been extremely successful in helping allowing companies to cope with multifaceted
risks caused by the distributed decision-making in their supply chains, especially
as they have become more global. Software ecosystems, similarly, represent distributed decisions in supply chains of code and author contributions, suggesting that
relationships among projects, developers, and source code have to be measured. We
then describe a massive measurement infrastructure involving discovery, extraction,
cleaning, correction, and augmentation of publicly available open-source data from
version control systems and other sources. We then illustrate how the key relationships among the nodes representing developers, projects, changes, and files can be
accurately measured, how to handle absence of measures for user base in version
control data, and, finally, illustrate how such measurement infrastructure can be used
to increase knowledge resilience in FLOSS.

S. Amreen · T. Dey · Y. Ma · A. Mockus (✉) · S. Mousavi
Department of Electrical Engineering and Computer Science, University of Tennessee,
Knoxville, TN 37996, USA
e-mail: audris@utk.edu

B. Bichescu · R. Bradley · R. Zaretzki
Haslam College of Business, University of Tennessee, Knoxville,
TN 37996, USA
e-mail: bbichescu@utk.edu

R. Bradley
e-mail: rbradley@utk.edu

R. Zaretzki
e-mail: rzaretzk@utk.edu

© Springer Nature Singapore Pte Ltd. 2019
B. Fitzgerald et al. (eds.), *Towards Engineering Free/Libre Open Source
Software (FLOSS) Ecosystems for Impact and Sustainability*,
https://doi.org/10.1007/978-981-13-7099-1_1

1.1 Introduction

Open source is, perhaps, the least understood among the revolutionary inventions of the humankind. This is, perhaps, not very surprising because just two decades ago it was a mere curiosity, yet now, with its exponential growth, it has reached all corners of the society. This lack of understanding, however, is not excusable because much of the societies critical infrastructure and the ability to innovate depend on the heath of Free/Libre and Open Source Software (FLOSS).

Here, we attempt to alleviate this gap in understanding by proposing a measurement infrastructure capable of encompassing the entire FLOSS ecosystem in the large. To do that, we start from introducing conceptual framework of supply chains and adapting it to the unique features of the FLOSS ecosystem. In particular, we define software supply chain as the collection of developers and software projects producing new versions of the source code. This supply chain analogy provides us with key concepts of the abstract network involving nodes that represent developers, changes, projects, and files. The production process involves creating new versions of files via atomic increments that deliver specific value (commits). We then proceed to operationalize these and additional concepts from bottom-up, i.e., from publicly available atomic records representing code changes.

The process of collecting and extracting this public data is involved due to lack of a single global registry of all FLOSS projects, the need to extract data from git database, need to store a petabyte of the data, and the need to convert it into a form so that the necessary measures could be calculated.

Before we can engage in the construction of the supply chain relationships, we need accurate identification of developers and projects and the relationships among them. Developers' identities are often misspelled, while projects may represent temporary forks of other projects. Both issues need to be addressed. Once the basic data has been cleaned and corrected in this way, we can engage in estimation of direct relationships that involve five basic types as given below:

- Authorship links file(s) modified with the author and includes basic data in a commit: date and commit message.
- Version history links changes (and, therefore, versions of a file) through a parent–child relationship with each commit having zero or more parent commits.
- Static dependence links source code files via package use or call-flow dependencies.
- Project inclusion links projects (VCS repositories) with changes and all versions of files contained therein.
- Code copy dependencies identify instances of code between specific versions of files and, in conjunction with version history, can be used to create Universal Version History that breaks project boundaries.

In combination, these dependencies induce additional networks, for example, the knowledge flow graph of developers connected trough files they modify in succession or upstream/downstream collaboration graph linking developers working on projects that have static dependencies.

Once the data for software supply chains is produced, the types of attributes that are directly available are limited and we, typically, need to augment basic data with quantities that may reside in other data sources, for example, responsiveness that resides in projects' issue trackers or Q&A websites, or may be entirely unavailable, for example, the number of end users and, therefore, has to be obtained from models.

Finally, we illustrate how the constructed measurements can be used to increase resilience of the FLOSS ecosystem to the knowledge loss by assigning observers or maintainers to the strategically selected projects or source code files.

The remainder of this chapter is organized as follows: In Sect. 1.2, the definition of FLOSS supply chains and general approaches used to optimize FLOSS supply chains' network are provided. In Sect. 1.3, the process of collecting and storing data from software projects hosted on various open-source platforms is described. Section 1.4 composed the data extraction process, storage, and cleaning through disambiguating author identities. Section 1.5 depicts operationalization of software supply chain by constructing code reuse, knowledge flow, and dependency networks. In Sect. 1.6, we provide a redundancy-based approach to have more maintainers responsible for in-danger-files to reduce the knowledge loss in the FLOSS ecosystem.

1.2 Supply Chains in FLOSS

The key output of software development activity is the source code. Therefore, software development is reflected in the way the source code is created and modified. Although various individual and groups of projects have been well studied, it only gives partial results and conclusions on the propagation and reuse of source code in the large. As in traditional supply chains, the developers in FLOSS make individual decisions with some cooperative action, and hence the analytical findings from traditional supply chains may help in FLOSS. Second, we have a complicated network of technical dependencies with code and knowledge flows akin to traditional supply chains, making the analogies less complicated. Third, the emerging phenomena, for example, the lack of transparency and visibility, appear to be as, or more, important in FLOSS as in traditional supply chains. Fourth, unlike traditional supply chains, FLOSS has very detailed information about the production and dependencies. We, therefore, hope that detailed data with supply chain analytical framework may bring transformative insights not just for FLOSS supply chains, but for all supply chains generally. We, therefore, would like to systematically analyze the entire network among all the repositories on all source forges, revealing upstream to downstream relations, the flow of code, and the flow of knowledge within and among projects.

1.2.1 Defining FLOSS Supply Network

La Londe et al. proposed a supply chain as a set of firms that pass materials forward [20], Lambert et al. define a supply chain as the alignment of firms that brings products or services to market [21], Christopher [8] described supply chain as the network of organizations that are involved, through upstream and downstream linkages, in the different processes and activities that produce value in the form of products and services delivered to the ultimate consumer. A common comprehension is that the supply chain is a set of three or more companies directly linked by one or more of the upstream or downstream flows of products, services, finance, and information from a source to a customer.

As software product developers increasingly depend on external suppliers, supply chains emerge, as in other industries. Upstream suppliers provide assets downstream to as more complex products emerge. As open-source software proliferates, developers of new software tend to build on top of mature projects or packages with only a small amount of modifications, which leads to the emergence of software supply chain in OSS.

A supply chain with individual developers and groups (software projects or packages) representing "companies" producing new versions of the source code (e.g., files, modules, frameworks, or entire distributions). The upstream and downstream flows from projects to end users is represented by the dependencies and sharing of the source code and by the contributions via patches, issues, and exchange of information. This is our definition of software supply chain. Supply chains lead to two important concepts.

Visibility is information that developers have about the inputs, processes, sources, and practices used to bring the product to consumers/market. This includes complete supply chain visibility including traceability for the entire supply chain. Visibility is, generally, inwardly/developer focused. Visibility refers to how far you can see upward beyond direct upstream, i.e., how many layers of dependency you can see from a software in supply chain.

Transparency is information that developers share with their consumers about the inputs, processes, sources, and practices used to bring the product to the consumer. It is more outwardly focused/from the consumer perspective than visibility. How much each the developer or project is providing publicly (including the ability to interpret that information by others) is a form of transparency.

1.2.2 Notation Used for FLOSS Supply Network

In traditional supply chain, producers are considered as nodes of a graph and the flow of information or materials as links. Based on the definition of software supply chain and the ability to measure it, we use the following notation for key concepts of software supply chain throughout the chapter:

1. A Node is a

   - Developer—an individual producer will be denoted as d. Developer author commits c with each commit having a single author $d = A(c)$.
   - A version of a file—a component work/information inserted into a project will be denoted as $f_v \in p$. File versions are produced by commits with each commit producing zero or more file versions.
   - Project—a group of commits (a composition of work by individual developers) in the same repository, it will be denoted as $p = \{c : c \in p\}$. Since each commit produces a set of file versions, a project is also associated with all these file versions: $p = \{f_v : f_v \in c, c \in p\}$ and all authors of the commits.

2. There are different types of links

   - A technical dependence (upstream/downstream project $l_d(p_1, p_2)$).
   - Code flow file, i.e., file that has been copied in the past but is now being maintained in parallel $l_c(f, f1) : \exists f1, v_i, v_j$ such that $f1_{v_j} = f_{v_i}$.
   - Authorship: $l_a(d, f) : \exists c$ such that $d = A(c) \wedge f_v \in c$.

1.3 Computing Infrastructure for Measuring FLOSS Supply Chains

FLOSS projects are not only scattered around the world, but they also tend to be scattered around the web, hence, in order to collect data for measurement we need to discover where the relevant data sources are located [27, 28]. Historically, a variety of version control and issue tracking tools were used, but many of the projects can be now found on a few large platforms like GitHub, BitBucket, SourceForge, and GitLab and most projects have converged to Git as their version control system.

1.3.1 Discovery

While many projects have moved to (or at least are mirrored on) the main forges such as GitHub, a sizable number of projects are hosted on other forges. The number of such forges is not small. Some of these do not have stable APIs and the rest requires a unique API to discover all public projects on that forge. This makes the task of gathering information from these forges fairly challenging. However, although collecting information from these sources require slightly different approaches (which makes it difficult to use one single script for mining), the task itself is not complicated and the only result required is the list of git URLs that could be used to mirror the data as described below. This makes the task an excellent candidate for crowdsourcing [25, 28]. Table 1.1 (from [25]) lists the active forges and an estimate of how many projects are hosted in each of them at the time of the study.

Table 1.1 Active forges (other than GitHub and BitBucket) with public repositories [25]

Forge name	Forge URL	API	Search method	Repositories retrieved
CloudForge	cloudforge.com	Private API	Google search	42
SourceForge	sourceforge.net	REST API	Google search	48,000–50,000
launchpad	launchpad.net	API	API	36,860
Assembla	assembla.com/home	No	Google search	about 70,000
CodePlex	codeplex.com	REST API	Google search	100,000
Savannah	savannah.gnu.org	No	Google search	3613
CCPForge	ccpforge.cse.rl.ac.uk/gf	No	Google search	126
Jenkins	ci.jenkins-ci.org	REST API	API	106,336
Repository Hosting	Respositoryhosting.com	No	Google search	<88
KForge	pythonhosted.org/kforge	API	python.org search	81,000
Phabricator	phabricator.org	Conduit API	API	about 10,000
Fedorahosted	fedorahosted.org/web	No	Google search	914
JavaForge	javaforge.com	No	Google search	7672
Kiln	fogcreek.com/kiln	No	Google search	43
SVNRepository	SVNRepository.com	No	Google search	15
Pikacode	pikacode.com	No	Google search	2
Planio	plan.io	No	Google search	26
GNA!	gna.org	No	Google search	1326
JoomlaCode	joomlacode.org/gf	REST API	Google search	971
tuxfamily	tuxfamily.org	No	Google search	209
pastebin	pastebin.com	No	Google search	about 1800
GitLab	gitlab.com	No	Google search	about 57,000
Eclipse	eclipse.org/home/index.php	No	Google search	214
Turnkey GNU	turnkeylinux.org/all	No	Google search	100
JavaNet	home.java.net/projects/alpha	No	Google search	1583
Stash	atlassian.com/software/bitbucket/server	REST API	API	5400
Transifex	transifex.com	No	Google search	5400
Tigris	tigris.org	No	Google search	678

Apart from discovering open-source projects from forges that host VCS, software projects information can also be found in the metadata of popular Linux distributions. In particular [28], Gentoo, Debian, Slackware, OpenSuse, and RedHat distributions and package repositories such as rpmforge provided a list of popular packages. Moreover, there are directories of open-source projects that list home page URLs and other information about the projects. RawMeat (no longer in operation) and Free Software

Foundation were two prominent examples of such directories. While they do not host VCSs or even provide URLs to a VCS, they do provide pointers to source code snapshots in tarballs and project home pages.

1.3.2 Retrieval, Extraction, and Schema for Analytics

Source code changes in software projects are recorded in a version control system (VCS). Git is presently the most common version control system, sometimes with historic data imported from SVN or other VCS used in the past. Code changes are typically organized into commits that make changes to one or more source code files. Git repositories hosted on open-source platforms can be retrieved by cloning them (functionality provided by `git clone -mirror`) to local servers.

The retrieved git database stores the full history of changes/commits made to a project. A Git commit records author, commit time, a pointer to the projects' file system, a pointer to the parent change, and the text of the commit message. Internally, the Git database has three primary types of objects: commits, trees, and blobs. Each object is represented by its sha1 value that can be used as a key to find its content. The content of a blob object is a content of a specific version of a file. The content of a tree object is a folder in a file system represented by the list of sha1s for the blobs and the trees (subfolders) contained in it. A commit contains sha1 for the corresponding tree, a list of parent commit sha1s, an author id, a committer id, a commit timestamp, and the commit message.

We extract git objects from each project and store them in the common database. This reduces the amount of storage needed approximately 100 times (which is an average number of projects a git object belongs to) and allows us to conduct analysis of the relationships. We have 2.8B blobs, 3.1B trees, and 0.8B commits collected from 40 million projects.

Git is not a system that stores data in a way that makes analysis easy. We, therefore, reorganize and restructure it in an efficient way to facilitate various analytics related to the above-described concepts of software supply chain. The data must be stored in a way that allows fast and efficient data lookup for billions of objects. An appropriate structure for that is a hashtable or a key-value database optimized to retrieve fast by exact value of a key. For example, in order to retrieve all commits made by a developer, the developer ID is stored as the key and the list of commits authored by the developer is stored as the value associated with that key. Another example is the link between a commit and files modified by the commit. This is accomplished by comparing the tree (and all subtrees) of the commit with the tree of the parent commit. The new blobs created indicate new f_vs. Since the complete tree and subtrees can be fairly large, the operation is computationally nontrivial and, because such relationships are commonly needed, is worth precomputing.

We compared the performance of several key-value databases and found that TokyoCabinet to be the most competitive one in terms of trade-offs between speed and storage needs. We break the keys by part of their sha1 into up to 128 different

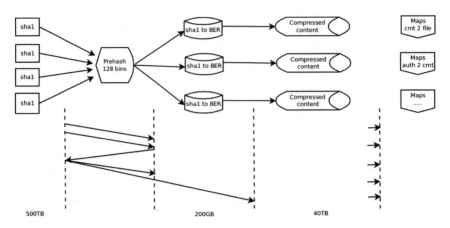

Fig. 1.1 Data retrieval diagram

databases to facilitate parallel (hadoop-like) processing when we need to iterate over the entire database and to reduce the size of each individual database. These key-value maps are constructed to map developers to authored commits and files, commits to projects (and back), commits to their children commits, blobs created (and back to commit), and other lookup tables needed to construct the software supply chain.

The overall diagram of the data workflow is shown in Fig. 1.1. The calendar time goes down, while the data layers from raw to analytics go from left to right.

1.4 Correction and Augmentation

Operational data extracted from software repositories [31] often contain incorrect and missing values. For example, and most importantly, primary author id, a key field for many analyses, often suffers from errors such as multiple or erroneous spellings, identity changes that occur over time, group identities, and other issues. These problems arise because primary author information in a Git commit (which we study here) depends on an entry specifying username and email in a Git configuration file for the specific computer a developer is using at the moment. Once the Git commit is recorded, it is immutable like other Git objects and cannot be changed. Once a developer pushes their commits from the local to remote repository, that author information remains. A developer may have multiple laptops, workstations, and work on various servers, and it is possible and, in fact, likely, that on at least one of these computers the Git configuration file has a different spelling of their name and email. It is also not uncommon to see the commits done under an organizational alias, thus obscuring the identity of the author.

Since developers serve as nodes in the supply chain network, it is of paramount importance to determine developer identities accurately. Erroneous data in developer identifiers can result in a misrepresented network undermining the value of constructing an OSS supply chain network. These issues have been recognized in software engineering [2, 12] and beyond [9]. However, identity resolution to identify actual developers based on data from software repositories is nontrivial mainly due to

1. Lack of ground truth—absence of validated maps from the recorded to actual identities. Similar disambiguation approaches have been applied on census data [9] or patent data [44], whereby over 150,000 samples of ground truth data were available.
2. Data Volume—millions of developer identities in hundreds of millions of code commits.

   To avoid these challenges, studies in the software engineering field tend to focus on individual projects or groups of projects where the number of IDs that need to be disambiguated is small enough for manual validation. Most traditional record matching techniques use string similarity of identifiers (typically login credentials), i.e., name, username, and email similarity. A broad spectrum of approaches ranging from direct string comparisons of name and email [2, 43] to supervised learning based on string similarity [44] have been used to solve the identity problem in the past. However, such methods do not resolve all issues that are particular to data generated by version control systems. Therefore, in order to propose solutions or to tailor existing identity resolution approaches, we need a better understanding of the nature of the errors associated with the records related to developer identity.

1.4.1   Problems with the Data

We inspected the collection of more than nine million author strings collected from over 500M Git commits and looked at random subsets of author IDs to understand how or why these errors occur. We identified these errors and broadly categorized them into the following three kinds—synonyms, homonyms, and missing data and determined the common reasons causing errors to be injected into the system.

1. Synonyms: These kinds of errors are introduced when a person uses different strings for names, user names, or email addresses. For example, "utsav dusad <utsavdusad@gmail.com>" and "utsavdusad <utsavdusad@gmail.com>" are identified as synonyms.
   Spelling mistakes such as "Paul Luse <paul.e.luse@intel.com>" and "paul luse <paul.e.luse@itnel.com>" are also classified as synonyms, as "itnel" is likely to be a misspelling of "intel". Developers may change their name over time, for example, after marriage, creating a synonym.
2. Homonyms: Homonym errors are introduced when multiple people use the same organizational email address. For example, the Id "saper <saper@saper.info>" may be used by multiple entities in the organization. For example "Marcin Cieslak

<saper@saper.info>" is an entity who may have committed under the above organizational alias.

Template credentials from tools is another source that might introduce homonym errors in the data as some users may not enter values for name and/or an email field. For example, "Your Name <vponomaryov@mirantis.com>" which may belong to author "vponomaryov <vponomaryov@mirantis.com>". Sometimes developers do not want their identities or their email address to be seen, resulting in intentionally anonymous name, such as John Doe or email, such as devnull@localhost.

3. Missing Data: Errors are also introduced when a user leaves the name or email field empty, for example, "chrisw <unknown>".

A look at the most common, names and user names shows that many of them were unlikely to be names of individuals. For example, the most frequent names in the dataset such as "nobody", "root", and "Administrator" are a result of homonym errors as shown in Table 1.2.

1.4.2 Disambiguation Approach

Traditional record linkage methodology and identity linking in software [2] split identity strings into several parts. Our approach splits the information in the author string into several fields representing the structure of that string and defines similarity metrics for all author pairs. We also incorporate the term frequency measure for each of the attributes in a pair. Finally, we add similarity between behavioral fingerprints for all pairs of authors in the dataset.

1. **Author Distances Based on String Similarity**: Each author string is stored in the following format—"name <email>", e.g., "Hong Hui Xiao <xiaohhui@cn.ibm.com>". For our analysis, we define the following attributes for each user:

   a. Author: String as extracted from source as shown in the example above.
   b. Name: String up to the space before the first "<".
   c. Email: String within the "<>" brackets.
   d. First name: String up to the first space, "+", "−", "_", ",", "." and camel case encountered in the name field.
   e. Last name: String after the last space, "+", "−", "_", ",", "." and camel case encountered in the name field.
   f. User name: String up to the "@" character in the email field.

Additionally, we introduce a field "inverse first name", whereby the last name of the author is assigned to this attribute. In the case where there is a string without any delimiting character in the name field, the first name and last name are replicated. For example, bharaththiruveedula <bharath_ves@hotmail.com> would have "bharaththiruveedula" replicated in the first, last, and the name field.

Table 1.2 Data overview: the 10 most frequent names and emails

Name	Count	First name	Count	Last name	Count	Email	Count	User name	Count
unknown	140859	unknown	140875	unknown	140865	<blank>	16752	root	72655
root	66905	root	66995	root	67004	none@none	9576	nobody	35574
nobody	35141	David	45091	nobody	35141	devnull@localhost	8108	github	19778
Ubuntu	18431	Michael	40199	Ubuntu	18560	student@epicodus.com	5914	ubuntu	18683
(no author)	6934	nobody	35142	Lee	10826	unknown	3518	info	18634
nodemcu-custom-build	6073	Daniel	34889	Wang	10641	you@example.com	2596	<blank>	17826
Alex	5602	Chris	29167	Chen	9792	anybody@emacswiki.org	2518	me	14312
System administrator	4216	Alex	28410	Smith	9722	=	1371	admin	12612
Administrator	4198	Andrew	26016	Administrator	8668	Unknown	1245	mail	11253
< blank >	4185	John	25882	User	8622	noreply	913	none	11004

In order to measure the distance between strings, we tested two common measures of string similarity, the Levenshtein score and the Jaro–Winkler score [47]. Our experiments indicated that the Jaro–Winkler similarity produces scores that are more reflective of actual similarity as verified by human experts than the Levenshtein score. Therefore, we implemented the Jaro–Winkler score as the measure of similarity throughout the rest of this study.

The Jaro Similarity is defined as

$$sim_j = \begin{cases} 0, & \text{if } m = 0 \\ \dfrac{1}{3}\left(\dfrac{m}{|s_1|} + \dfrac{m}{|s_2|} + \dfrac{m-t}{m}\right) & \text{otherwise} \end{cases}$$

where s_i is the length of string i, m is the number of matching characters, and t is half the number of transpositions.

The Jaro–Winkler similarity modifies the Jaro similarity so that differences at the beginning of the string have more significance than differences at the end. It is defined as

$$sim_w = sim_j + lp(1 - sim_j)$$

where l is the length of a common prefix at the start of the string up to a maximum of four characters and p ($<=0.25$) is a scaling factor for how much the score is adjusted upward for having common prefixes.

2. **Author Distance Based on String Frequency**: We count the number of occurrences of the attributes for each author as defined in Sect. 1.4.2, i.e., name, first name, last name, user name, and email for our dataset. We calculate the similarity between author pairs, authors a_1 and a_2, for each of these attributes as follows:

$$f_{sim} = \begin{cases} \log_{10} \dfrac{1}{f_{a_1} \times f_{a_2}} & \text{if } a_1 \text{ and } a_2 \text{ are valid} \\ -10 & \text{otherwise} \end{cases}$$

We generate a list of 200 common strings of names, first names, last names, usernames, and emails from the larger dataset of 9.4M authors (the first 10 shown in Table 1.2) and manually remove names that appear to be legitimate, i.e., Lee, Chen, Chris, Daniel, etc. We set string frequency similarity of a pair of name or first name or last name or username to -10 if at least one element of the pair belongs a string identified as not legitimate. This was done in order to let the learning algorithm recognize the difference between the highly frequent strings and strings that are not useful as author identifiers. We found that the value for other highly frequent terms was significantly greater than -10.

3. **Author Distances Based on Fingerprints**: There are four additional distance measures we incorporate into our study which address the behavioral attributes of authors: (1) Author similarity based on files touched, when two authors identities have modified the same files there is a greater chance that they represent the same entity. (2) Author similarity based on time zone, two author identities committing

in the same time zone indicate geographic proximity and, therefore, a higher similarity weight is given. (3) Author similarity based on text, similarity in style of text between two author identities may indicate that they are the same physical entity. (4) Gender incorporating gender information helps us distinguish between highly similar author identity strings. Quantitative operationalizations are given below:

a. **Author similarity based on files touched**: Each file is weighted using the number of authors who has modified it. The file weight is defined as the inverse of the number of distinct authors who have modified that file. The pairwise similarity between authors, a_1 and a_2, is derived by summing over the weights of the files touched by both authors. A similar metric was found to work well finding instances of succession (when one developer takes over the work of another developer) [29]. In this metric, we consider only the first 100 common authors for a given file.

$$file\_weight(W_f) = \frac{1}{A_f}, \text{ where } A = |a_1, \ldots, a_n|$$

$$ad_{a_1a_2} = \sum_{i=1}^{n_{a_1a_2}} W_{f_i}, \text{ where } n_{a_1a_2} = |f_{a_1} \cap f_{a_2}|$$

b. **Author similarity based on time zone**: We discovered 300 distinct time-zone strings from the commits and created a "author by time zone" matrix that had the count of commits by an author in a given time zone. All time zones that had less than two entries were eliminated from further study. Each author is therefore assigned a normalized time-zone vector (with 139 time zones) that represents the pattern of his commits. Similar to the previous metric, we weighted each time zone by the inverse number of authors who committed at least once in that time zone. We multiply each author's time-zone vector by the weight of the time zone. We define author i's time-zone vector as

$$a_i = C_{a_i} \cdot \frac{1}{A_T},$$

Here, C_{a_i} is the vector representing the commits of an author i in the different time zones and A_T is the vector representing the number of authors in the different time zones. The pairwise similarity metric between author a_1 and author a_2 is calculated as follows:

$$tzd_{a_1a_2} = cos\_sim(a_1, a_2)$$

where a_1 and a_2 are the authors' respective vectors.

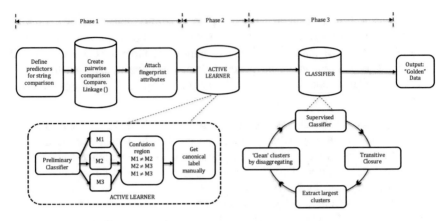

Fig. 1.2 Concept of the disambiguation process

   c. **Text similarity**: We use the Gensim's[1] implementation of the Doc2Vec [22] algorithm to generate vectors that embed the semantics and style of the commits messages of each author. All commit messages for each individual who contributed at least once to one of the OpenStack projects were gathered from the collection described above and a Doc2Vec model was built. We obtained a 200-dimensional vector for each of the 16,007 authors in our dataset and calculated cosine similarity to find pairwise similarity between authors.

$$d2v_{a_1a_2} = cos\_sim(a_1, a_2)$$

   d. **Gender Similarity**: We obtain the gender of the users as either Male, Female, or Undetermined. The similarity between author pairs are determined as follows:

$$gs_{a_1a_2} = \begin{cases} 0.5, & \text{if } G_{a_1} \text{ or } G_{a_2} = \text{Undetermined} \\ 1, & \text{if } G_{a_1} = G_{a_2} \\ 0, & \text{if } G_{a_1} \neq G_{a_2} \end{cases}$$

where G_i represents the gender of author i.

4. **Data Correction**: The data correction process can be divided into three broad phases as shown in Fig. 1.2.

   a. **Define predictors**—In this phase, we compute the string similarity, frequency similarity, and behavioral similarity. We use functions from the RecordLinkage library [41] to compute Jaro–Winkler similarities of the defined attributes (name, first name, last name, email, username). We com-

---

[1] https://radimrehurek.com/gensim/index.html.

pute string similarity between a pair of authors' name, first name, last name, username, email, and the first author's first name to the second author's last name (we refer to this as the inverse first name). Based on our preliminary analysis, we found many instances of developers using their names in both orders. In addition to the string similarities based on these fields, we also include the term frequency metric, as is commonly done in record matching literature. The high-frequency values tend to carry less discriminative power than infrequent email addresses or names. Finally, we include three finger-print metrics—author similarity based on files touched, time-zone similarity, and commit log text similarity. This resulting matrix data is used as an input to the next phase, the active learning process.

b. **Active learning**—This phase uses a preliminary classifier to extract a small set from large collection of data and generate labels for further classification. Supervised classification requires ground truth data. As noted earlier, it is extremely time-consuming and error prone to produce a large set of manually classified data to serve as an input for a supervised classifier. Moreover, identifying a small subset of instances so that the classifier would produce accurate results on the remainder of the data is also challenging. A concept called *Active Learning* [40] using a preliminary classifier helps us extract a small set of author pairs that is viable for manual labeling, from the set of over 256M author pairs. To design the preliminary classifier, we partition the data into ten parts and fit bootstrap aggregation (bagging) models on three different combinations of nine parts and predict on one of the ten parts. Each classifier learns from manually classified pairs and outputs links or non-links for each author pair in the prediction set. The three classifiers trained on different training subsets yield slightly different predictions (links and non-links for each pair). The mismatch between predictions of two such classifiers indicates instances where the classifier has large uncertainty (confusion regions). We conducted a probabilistic manual classification on the cases in the confusion region of the classifier and extracted pairs where links were assigned with full confidence, i.e., probability $= 1$. Each pair was updated manually to include a canonical label chosen from among the existing author identities that had a proper name and email address. This produces a preliminary set of training data for supervised classification.

c. **Classification**—In this phase, we discuss supervised classification suitable for disambiguation, transitive closure applied on classifier output, extraction of clusters to correct, and disaggregation of wrongly clustered individuals. Once the labeled dataset is created, we use it to train random forest models which are commonly used in record matching literature. A 10-fold cross-validation using this method produced high precision and recall scores for the classifier. The final predictor involves a transitive closure on the pairwise links obtained from the classifier.[2] The result of the transitive closure is a set of connected components with each cluster representing a single physical entity. Once the clusters are obtained, we consider all clusters containing 10 or more elements since a significant portion of such clusters had multiple developers grouped into a single component. The resulting 20 clusters—44 elements in the largest and 10 elements in the smallest cluster among these— were then manually inspected and grouped. This manual effort included the assessment of name, username, and email similarity, projects they worked on, as well as looking up individual's profiles online if names/emails were not sufficient to assign them to a cluster with adequate confidence.

1.4.3 Handling Missing Data

In addition to the bad and/or incorrect data, the observational data collected for the different software ecosystems often do not have observations for all the relevant variables [31, 48]. Generally, the missing data problem focuses on cases where a few observation values are missing for an otherwise observed variable [24], however, when talking about missing data in this context, we have to take into consideration cases where a number of variables might be completely unobserved as well. For example, if we are trying to measure the popularity of a particular project in an ecosystem, the best possible measure would be the number of active users. However, the number of active users is a quantity very hard to measure in practice, and the second-best measure, the number of downloads, is typically not tracked very accurately for most FLOSS software. At this point, our choices are to either find a proxy measure for the popularity of a project or find a way to estimate the unobserved variables.

As for the proxy measures, there are a few options, e.g., the number of stars/ watchers/forks for a GitHub project [16, 37, 45], however, although these measures should closely correlate with the actual popularity of the product, sometimes analyses done using these measures could end up finding some relationship that is an artifact related to that particular measure, and is not reflective of the actual popularity. Because these metrics are easily manipulated, they may also be deliberately biased and not representative.

A more appealing option, therefore, is to estimate the missing observations. In the more common case of missing data estimation, only a few observations are missing for a variable, and the estimation can be done by means of partial/full imputation and/or interpolation or extrapolation [24]. However, when a variable is completely unobserved for a dataset, such techniques cannot be used. In such a scenario, a set of alternative methods are useful, as listed below:

---

[2]We found that more accurate predictors can be obtained by training the learner only on the matched pairs, since the transitive closure typically results in some pairs that are extremely dissimilar, leading the learner to learn from them and predict many more false positives.

- **Factor analysis** [11, 13, 26]: If we have measures for a set of variables that are likely to be affected by a common set of unobserved variables, we can perform a method called factor analysis on the observed variables to extract an estimate for the missing unobserved "factors". This method, however, depends on both a parametric probability model and assumes a particular relationship between the unobserved variables and the multivariate observation.

  With regard to the example of measuring the popularity (i.e., number of users) of a project, if we have measurements for a set of variables (hypothetically) directly affected by the number of users (e.g., number of crashes, downloads, or even forks or stars for a GitHub project), we can extract the maximum likelihood factors from those variables (e.g., by using the `factanal` function in R[3]), which, under the assumption that each observation is the sum of a linear combination of the underlying missing factors and a Gaussian noise component, should give an accurate estimate of the number of users.

- **Prediction**: If the scenario is such that the values of a variable are available only in certain situations, a predictive model can be used for estimating the unobserved variable. For example, the number of users for a particular software might be available only for a specific subset of releases. In this case, we may use the complete observations for releases where the data is observed to train a model (e.g., linear regression model or Random Forest) that can be used to predict the number users in cases where this quantity is not observed.

- **Hidden node detection using graphical models**: If a graphical model is used for modeling the interrelationship among the variables, an unobserved variable might be represented by a hidden node in the graph and can be estimated using data from the variables that have connections to the hidden node [15, 17, 35]. Factor analysis may be viewed as a special case of this type of analysis.

  In order to measure the number of users for a software in this method, we first need to construct a graphical model of dependence among all of the observed variables. Two strategies are usually used to define the structure: (1) the graph represents dependencies obtained from domain experts or (2) the graph may initially be based on prior distributions about the parameters of the overall model. The data is then used to calculate the posterior distribution and to make inference. The second approach makes minimal a priori assumptions about the model and focuses on the search for the best graphical representation for a given dataset (structure learning). This is an NP-hard problem [7], but a number of different heuristic structure learning algorithms are available [42].

  After the model is constructed, one or more hidden nodes can be added to it. The standard approach is adding one node at a time and optimizing its placement by optimizing the network score (generally BIC score in such situations) at each step [4, 14].

  Graphical models have several advantages over regression models. To be precise, regression analysis is a very simple graphical model allowing one directed link from each independent variable to dependent variable. Therefore, the more

---

[3]https://www.statmethods.net/advstats/factor.html.

general approach of graphical models can help with multicollinearity (which is a common problem in the software due to many of the observed variables being highly correlated) by linking independent variables.

1.5   Code and Knowledge Flow and Technical Dependencies

The most fundamental part of software supply chain or ecosystem is the networks of dependencies and code or knowledge flows. **The dependency network** is based on technical dependencies. These can be subdivided into several types. For example, a runtime dependency requires a library from another package to be available when the program is run. Package dependencies in Debian are an example of such relationship. A different type of dependency is build dependency, where a set of tools and include files may be needed in order to compile and build a package. Optional dependencies usually denote the potential extension in the functionality of a program if that dependency is satisfied. **The code flow network** represents the source code copying. **The knowledge flow network** represents implicit exchange of information as developers modify source code in sequence. A senior developer d_s creates (or modifies) a set of source code files. Another developer d_j modifies a subset of these files, thus having to understand design decisions made by d_s. This mentor–follower knowledge flow can be quantified [29].

1.5.1   Constructing Technical Dependencies

As discussed above, different types of technical dependencies exist. Major types are dependencies required to run software and dependencies required to build software. Each dependency may need to be obtained differently for projects that are inside package managers such as deb or npm (and, thus, have metadata in the package manager that explicitly specifies the dependencies) and projects outside package managers, where dependencies can only be extracted based on the actual content of the code, configuration, and build scripts.

Dependencies within a specific package manager are recorded when a new package is added into package manager or its dependencies change. For example, the dependency information for packages hosted on NPM can be extracted from PACKGE.json file and is also stored in the NPM registry.

Different package managers may have different standards of defining dependencies, e.g., NPM has five types of dependencies: dependencies, devDependencies, peerDependencies, bundledDependencies, and optionalDependencies, while packages in R CRAN also have five (but not equivalent) types: depends, imports, suggests, linkingto, and enhances. Defining standards for the categorization of dependencies that are generally applicable to all package managers may not be possible.

We illustrate the procedures of constructing the dependency network by exploring R CRAN ecosystem. R package can be scraped from R CRAN official website which contains approximately 11K packages. We used data from METACRAN[4] which provides the latest R CRAN metadata containing the dependency information. As we have mentioned in the introduction, there are five types of dependency keywords in R CRAN and we considered "imports" and "depends" as dependency, because packages listed in "imports" must be installed in advance and "depends"[5] is the old name for "imports".

By creating a link from individual package to each dependency in its "imports" and "depends", we construct a dependency network for R CRAN in Fig. 1.3. Packages with degree less than 20 are removed which ends up with 421 (1.9%) nodes and 3235 (6.6%) edges in Fig. 1.3. Node size is proportional to its betweenness centrality value and the color is based on modularization algorithm[6] of gephi. In Fig. 1.3, numerous dependency links are revealed among popular R CRAN packages. In particular, "ggplot2", "Hmisc", "reshape2", "stringr", and "Rcpp" are core packages based on betweenness centrality.

Unfortunately, projects that are not a part of the registries of package managers may have no metadata that allows easy identification of dependencies. Since such projects represent a bulk of projects, the dependencies need to be extracted directly from the source/configuration/build code. For example, import statements in Java or Python, use statements in Perl, include statement in C, or, as is the case for our study, library statements for the R-language.

Below is an example workflow to determine dependencies for all R files in all projects:

1. Identify all R-language files by extension (.r or .R) in the complete list of all files in the file-to-commit map described above.

2. For each filename use filename-to-blob (file versions) map to obtain the content for all versions of the R-language files obtained in Step 1.

3. Analyze the resulting set of blobs to find a statement indicating an install or a use of a package:

- `install\.packages\(.*"PACKAGE".*\)`
- `library\(.*[\"']*?PACKAGE[\"']*?.*\)`
- `require\(.*[\"']*?PACKAGE[\"']*?.*\)`

4. Use blob-to-commit map to obtain all commits that produced these blobs and then use the commit to determine the date that the blob was created.

5. Use commit-to-project map to gather all projects that installed the relevant set of packages.

A similar approach can be applied to other languages and technologies with suitable modification in the dependency extraction procedures, since different package

---

[4]METACRAN is a collection of services around the CRAN repository of R packages. https://www.r-pkg.org/about.

[5]Prior to the rollout of namespaces in R 2.14.0, Depends was the only way to "depend" on another package. Now, despite the name, you should almost always use Imports, not Depends.

[6]https://github.com/gephi/gephi/wiki/Modularity.

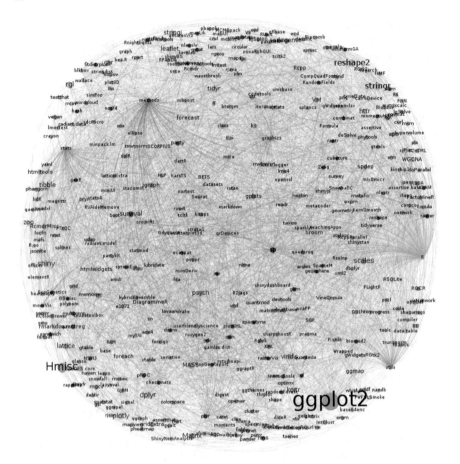

Fig. 1.3 R CRAN dependency network

managers, different languages, or different frameworks might require alternative approaches to identify dependencies or the instances of use. Dependencies can typically be detected in a programming language or build system-dependent manner [39]. For example, the dependency information of a Python source file is listed in `import` statement; dependency information of a C project is listed in header files; package dependency in Debian can be extracted by *apt-cache depends package-name*.

1.5.2   Constructing Code Flow Networks

In FLOSS, the code sharing is possible and welcome, unlike in proprietary software and is, perhaps, one of the key advantages that brings rapid innovation with new projects building from components or copied code of existing projects.

Code flow has been extensively investigated, albeit at a smaller scale. To determine instances of code flow several approaches may be taken as given below:

- Compare the strings representing the content of a source code file in the potential source and the potential destination [1, 18, 19].
- Compare the strings representing the file name and the path [5, 6, 50].

Here, we illustrate the first approach as it is largely language independent and allows detection for code and non-code flows. When two files have a matching content, i.e., $\exists v_1, v_2 : f_{v_1}^1 = f_{v_2}^2$ and f^1 and f^2 are files from distinct projects, it is not unreasonable to assume that $f_{v_1}^1$ and $f_{v_2}^2$ were not created independently but the code was copied. This applies if the unit of code is not an entire file, but only a part of file. From the theoretical perspective, we may produce false links (links where code flow does not exist, i.e., the content of both files was created independently of each other) and also miss links where information does flow, as in cases where the copied code was modified substantially before being committed to the repository.

We, therefore, need to quantify and minimize both of these potential errors. Whether we look at the file content or file pathname, the erroneous links may be introduced if the two linked strings are similar (or the same) purely by chance and the information was never shared. If we assume the string to be a random sequence of characters, the chance that two strings of length n would match purely by chance is m^{-n} where m is the size of alphabet. We can easily eliminate false matches (make the chance of such matches negligibly small) by ensuring that the string is of nontrivial length. For example, a random string with ten characters (from alphabet of 26 letters) would match by chance with probability lower than 10^{-14}. By considering links that are based on strings exceeding such length we can ensure a very low probability of false matches.

Unfortunately, the strings representing file content and file pathnames are not random for a variety of reasons [6, 27, 50], which are as follows:

- file depth in a project is not randomly distributed (usually file depth varies between 2 to 5),
- filenames are not always related to file content, e.g., foo,
- some filenames are quite common among projects, e.g., main.c,
- the content may be generated by a tool, and therefore anyone using a tool will have exactly the same content, and
- the template may have been used and only small parts of the template have been modified.

We, therefore, have to add additional ways of eliminating false links from the supply chain network through other means. For example, by identifying the reasons for false positives and removing links that are similar to the identified reasons for false positives.

Once the presence of the link is established, the next question involves the direction of the code flow. *File creation time* may serve such purpose. For Case 1, if the creation time of file f_i precedes that of f_j the direction of flow should, in general, go from p_1

to p_2. For Case 2, if the matching version of file $f_i(v_i)$ was created prior to $f_j(v_j)$, the direction of flow should go from p_1 to p_2.

The rationale for such approach would be that if a file F is first created in Project A and then copied to Project B, the creation time of file F in Project A is prior than that in Project B, the Project B is likely to be downstream to Project A because file F was supplied to Project B from Project A. It is possible that in some cases the primary maintenance of file F may be transferred to Project B and Project A gets updates of file F from Project B, but such instances could be detected by a more in-depth analysis of version history of file F in both projects [5].

A detailed procedure to illustrate the constructing code flow network is discussed next.

1.5.2.1   Code Flow Network for ember.js

Front-side web framework ember.js has been attracting many contributors over several years, which makes it suitable to illustrate how complicated code flow network may be.

To create the code flow network, we first collect all file names f and file versions f_v in the form of their SHA1 digests from emberjs/ember.js project (E). We use project-To-filename map to obtain files $A = f \in E$ and project-To-blob map to obtain the file versions $B = f_v \in E$. For each file in A, we then use filename-To-project map to find all other projects that contain this file name. Similarly, for each $f_v \in B$, we use blob-To-project map to find all other projects that contain this blob. This procedure creates links from E to all projects that share a filename or a blob.

These initial links contain numerous false positives and need to be filtered. Links created by file names that start with a period are often created by IDE tools or programming language/script, so they should be removed as they do represent code transfer from one project to another. It represents not code flow, but dependence on the tool.

Links that are created by forked projects of Emberjs/ember.js also need to be removed because they are a part of Emberjs/ember.js project. GitHub forks are created primarily to be able to contribute to the main project via pull requests, not to start a new project. Again, these projects represent private branches and do represent code flow but at a finer granularity than we consider at the moment.

In addition to the traditional definition of a forked project where the development is done in parallel with no intention to merge projects, the repository of the code for Ubuntu/Debian distribution does represent an example of downstream development done in order to maintain compatibility among the projects collected into a single distribution.

Once false positives are eliminated, 54 projects have code flow to project from ember.js. To understand the patterns of code flow, we categorized these projects into different groups as follows:

- Build tools: rake—makefile for Ruby on Rails.
- Testing: qunit—a testing framework.
- Runtime: jQuery—a JavaScript library.
- Framework: epf—emberjs Persistence Foundation.
- Prior incarnations: SproutCore/Amber.js—early name for the emberjs project.
- Hard forks: innoarch/bricks.ui—a hard fork of emberjs that was then developed as a separate project.
- Tutorials: cookbooks/nodjs—early code examples.
- Package manager: package.json—a file for NPM package manager.

As we can see, these types of code flow have different causes: tools, libraries and frameworks, hard forks, documentation templates, and distribution templates. Each type of code flow appears, therefore, to represent different phenomena and needs to be identified and investigated separately.

1.5.3   Constructing Knowledge Flow Networks

Developer knowledge varies from developer to developer and depends on what they have worked on [10, 32]. A unit of work can be considered as experience atom [32] and approximated by developers' modifications to the source code. Each time a developer makes a change to a file, they have first to understand the design decisions that went to the code they modify and, at the same time, their modification (be it a code fix or additional functionality) implements their knowledge in the way the change is designed and implemented. Thus, the knowledge of earlier developers, through code, flows to developers who modify the code later. This observation can facilitate linking of developers through the timing of the changes they make on files modified in common. Using notation introduced above, let d_s, d_j denote two developers. Let F_{d_s, d_j} be a set of files modified by both developers. Let S_2 be the strength of expertise transferred. Let $N_{f d_s}$ be the number of changes developer d_s made to file f (changes are made and counted through commits). Let $FC(f, d_s)$ denote the time when developer d_s made his/her first change to file f. Then, the challenge of measuring the strength of knowledge flow from senior developer to his/her subsequent developers can be approximated via the following expression [29]:

$$S_2(d_s, d_j) = \sum_{\substack{f: \begin{cases} f \in F_{d_s, d_j} \\ FC(f, d_j) > FC(f, d_s) \end{cases}}} \frac{N_{f d_s} + N_{f d_j}}{\sum_i N_{f d_i}} \tag{1.1}$$

The formula can be interpreted as follows: the strength of expertise flow from developer d_s to developer d_j is based on the sum of their contribution ratio to files in which developer d_s's first change is earlier than developer d_j's. Files changed mostly by others where the two developers had contributed little would not contribute much

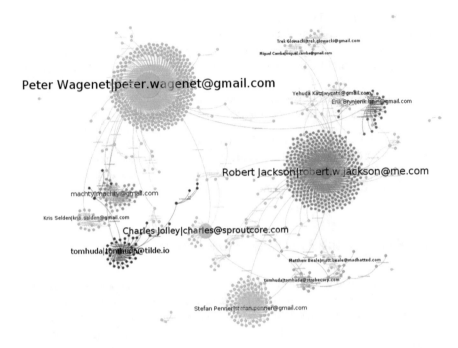

Peter Wagenet|peter.wagenet@gmail.com

Trek Glowacki|trek.glowacki@gmail.com

Miguel Camba|miguel.camba@gmail.com

Yehuda Katz|wycats@gmail.com

Erik Bryn|erik.bryn@gmail.com

Robert Jackson|robert.w.jackson@me.com

machty|machty@gmail.com

Kris Selden|kris.selden@gmail.com

Charles Jolley|charles@sproutcore.com

tomhuda|tomhuda@tilde.io

Matthew Beale|matt.beale@madhatted.com

tomhuda|tomhuda@strobecorp.com

Stefan Penner|stefan.penner@gmail.com

Fig. 1.4 Knowledge flow network for Emberjs

to the measure, but files where at least one developer made significant fraction of changes would contribute a lot.

For example, knowledge flow network in a popular web front-side framework—emberjs is shown in Fig. 1.4. The node size is proportional to its betweenness centrality value and the color is based on modularization algorithm[7] of gephi. Note that several labels have been adjusted to fit the page size. The most productive developers are annotated via their name and email. More information on ember.js can be found in 1.5.2.1. In Fig. 1.4, there are several big clusters of developers centered around each core developer. More specifically, "Peter Wagenet" and "Robert Jackson" are leading developers with vast number of successors. Clusters are linked by shared followers although the density of such links is low, indicating that majority of developers in ember.js tend to follow the work of a single-core developer.

---

[7]https://github.com/gephi/gephi/wiki/Modularity.

1.6   Example Application: Increasing Knowledge Redundancy

As developers who author source code become experts for that code, what happens if they, for some reason, stop maintaining the project? Fixing bugs or adding functionality to such code will become harder and fault prone [3, 29, 30, 34]. If an organization can identify the files that are likely to be left with no maintainer in the future, it may choose to assign their employees as additional maintainers to reduce the risk. It would seem that increasing the number (redundancy) of maintainers may reduce the risk. It may be possible to increase this knowledge redundancy by borrowing ideas from data redundancy. Erasure codes are forward error corrections codes used to prevent stored data from being lost by increasing data redundancy [36, 46]. Many improvements on erasure codes have been studied over the years [23, 33]. The main idea of the erasure codes is that the data of size B is divided into k segments and then the k segments are further converted into n segments such that $n = k + m$, where m is the amount of redundancy added to the original data. As a result, up to m segment failures can be tolerated.

Adding redundancy to the existing knowledge for each file can help mitigate the risk of lost knowledge resulting from developer turnover [38, 49]. Let us denote files as f, assigned maintainers as m, and original developers as d. Let us assume that we have I files, J developers, and Z backup maintainers.

We represent developer d_j and file f_i relationship as a developer matrix

$$D_{d_j f_i} = \begin{cases} 1 \ if \ d_j \ maintains \ f_i \\ 0 \qquad\qquad otherwise \end{cases}$$

For illustration, we include an example below, where developer d_1 is responsible for file f_1 but is not responsible for file f_2. Then, M is

$$D = \begin{bmatrix} & f_1 \ f_2 \ f_3 \ \cdots \ f_I \\ d_1: & 1 \ \ 0 \ \ 1 \ \cdots \ 1 \\ d_2: & 0 \ \ 1 \ \ 1 \ \cdots \ 0 \\ & \vdots \\ d_J: & 0 \ \ 0 \ \ 1 \ \cdots \ 0 \end{bmatrix}$$

Then, the number of developers responsible for file f_i is the sum of the column corresponding to file f_i, which in the example above, assuming d_3-$d_{(J-1)}$ are not maintaining any files, is

$$R = \begin{bmatrix} f_1 \ f_2 \ f_3 \ \cdots \ f_I \\ 1 \ \ 1 \ \ 3 \ \cdots \ 1 \end{bmatrix}$$

We refer to this vector R as knowledge redundancy.

Once the risky files (with low knowledge redundancy) are identified, the next step in our risk-mitigation approach is to assign the files at risk to backup maintainers. Let us define a threshold t that represents the maximum number of files that each backup maintainer is capable of being responsible for. We also define r as the minimum amount of redundancy that can be tolerated. Similar to matrix M above, we construct matrix M' for the backup maintainers, in which each row is a vector representing the files that the corresponding backup maintainer is responsible for.

$$M' = \begin{bmatrix} & f_1 & f_2 & f_3 & \cdots & f_I \\ m_1 : & 1 & 1 & 0 & \cdots & 1 \\ & & & \vdots & & \\ m_Z : & 0 & 1 & 1 & \cdots & 1 \end{bmatrix}$$

Files with fewer than r developers need one or more backup maintainers, but the sum of each row of M' cannot exceed the maintainer capacity threshold t. We first calculate the number of file/maintainer slots that need to be assigned to the backup maintainers. That number is $slots = rI - \sum_{i=1...I} \min(R_i, r)$. Obviously, we need at least $\max(r - \min_i r_i, slots/t)$ maintainers. To minimize the number of backup maintainers, we can always target the current maintainers to be responsible for some of the files that they are not currently in charge of, or count on volunteers.

The problem of optimally assigning files to backup maintainers can be cast as a mathematical integer program. Below is a possible formulation that can be solved with readily available solvers such as *CPLEX* or *Gurobi*.

$$\text{maximize} \sum_{i=1}^{I} R_i$$
$$\text{subject to} \sum_{i=1}^{J} M[i][j] + \sum_{z=1}^{Z} M'[z][j] \geq r, \; j = 1, \ldots, I$$
$$and$$
$$\sum_{i=1}^{I} M'[z][i] \leq t, \; z = 1, \ldots, Z$$

We can refine the objective to minimize the average or maximum risk resulting from discontinued contribution r developers together by adding conditions that are based on the structural properties of M. Using this approach, it is possible to increase the knowledge redundancy of each file to at least r (e.g., some file might already have more that r maintainers).

1.7 Conclusions

The ability to understand software ecosystems is limited by the ability to measure the relevant properties of these ecosystems and the conceptual framework needed to do the measurement. Many of the modeling or intervention techniques described in this book need a sound measurement framework. We have argued for the need to look at FLOSS from a global perspective and through the supply chain conceptual framework. We describe a concrete way to obtain highly detailed data of the entire FLOSS ecosystem, described ways to clean, correct, and augment basic version control data with metrics needed to produce knowledge and code flow networks and create models that, through increased visibility, can help developers and organizations make better decisions resulting in a healthy and productive FLOSS ecosystem.

References

1. I.D. Baxter, A. Yahin, L. Moura, M. Sant'Anna, L. Bier, Clone detection using abstract syntax trees, in *1998 Proceedings of International Conference on Software Maintenance* (IEEE, 1998), pp. 368–377
2. C. Bird, A. Gourley, P. Devanbu, M. Gertz, A. Swaminathan, Mining email social networks, in *Proceedings of the 2006 International Workshop on Mining Software Repositories, MSR '06* (ACM, New York, NY, USA, 2006), pp. 137–143
3. C. Bird, N. Nagappan, P. Devanbu, H. Gall, B. Murphy, Putting it all together: using socio-technical networks to predict failures, in *17th International Symposium on Software Reliability Engineering (ISSRE 09)*, Bengaluru-Mysuru, India, 2009
4. W.L. Buntine, Operations for learning with graphical models. J. Artif. Intell. Res. **2**, 159–225 (1994)
5. H.-F. Chang, A. Mockus, Constructing universal version history, in *ICSE'06 Workshop on Mining Software Repositories*, Shanghai, China, 22–23 May 2006, pp. 76–79
6. H.-F. Chang, A. Mockus, Evaluation of source code copy detection methods on FreeBSD, in *5th Working Conference on Mining Software Repositories*, ACM Press, 10–11 May 2008
7. D.M. Chickering, Learning bayesian networks is np-complete. Learn. Data: Artif. Intell. Stat. V **112**, 121–130 (1996)
8. M.L. Christopher, *Logistics and Supply Chain Management* (Pitman Publishing, London, 1992)
9. W.W. Cohen, P. Ravikumar, S.E. Fienberg, A comparison of string metrics for matching names and records, in *KDD Workshop on Data Cleaning and Object Consolidation*, 2003
10. T. Fritz, G.C. Murphy, E. Murphy-Hill, J. Ou, E. Hill, Degree-of-knowledge: modeling a developer's knowledge of code. ACM Trans. Softw. Eng. Methodol. (TOSEM) **23**(2), 14 (2014)
11. B. Fruchter, *Introduction to Factor Analysis* (Princeton, New York, 1954)
12. D. German, A. Mockus, Automating the measurement of open source projects, in *Proceedings of the 3rd Workshop on Open Source Software Engineering*, 2003, pp. 63–67
13. R.L. Gorsuch, Common factor analysis versus component analysis: some well and little known facts. Multivar. Behav. Res. **25**(1), 33–39 (1990)
14. D. Heckerman, A tutorial on learning with bayesian networks. Microsoft Research, 1995
15. K. Hornik, F. Leisch, A. Zeileis, Jags: a program for analysis of bayesian graphical models using gibbs sampling, in *Proceedings of DSC*, vol. 2, 2003, pp. 1–1
16. O. Jarczyk, B. Gruszka, S. Jaroszewicz, L. Bukowski, A. Wierzbicki, Github projects. quality analysis of open-source software, in *International Conference on Social Informatics* (Springer, Berlin, 2014), pp. 80–94
17. M.I. Jordan, *Learning in Graphical Models*, vol. 89 (Springer Science & Business Media, Berlin, 1998)
18. T. Kamiya, S. Kusumoto, K. Inoue, Ccfinder: a multilinguistic token-based code clone detection system for large scale source code. IEEE Trans. Softw. Eng. **28**(7), 654–670 (2002)
19. M. Kim, V. Sazawal, D. Notkin, G. Murphy, An empirical study of code clone genealogies, in *ACM SIGSOFT Software Engineering Notes*, vol. 30, (ACM, 2005), pp. 187–196

20. B.J. La Londe, J.M. Masters, Emerging logistics strategies: blueprints for the next century. Int. J. Phys. Distrib. Logist. Manag. **24**(7), 35–47 (1994)
21. D.M. Lambert, J.R. Stock, L.M. Ellram, *Fundamentals of Logistics Management* (McGraw-Hill/Irwin, New York, 1998)
22. Q. Le, T. Mikolov, Distributed representation of sentences and documents, in *Proceedings of the 31st International Conference on Machine Learning*, vol. 32 (JMLR, Beijing, China, 2014)
23. J. Li, X. Tang, C. Tian, A generic transformation to enable optimal repair in mds codes for distributed storage systems. IEEE Trans. Inf. Theory **64**(9), 6257–6267 (2018)
24. R.J.A. Little, D.B. Rubin, *Statistical Analysis with Missing Data* (Wiley, New Jersey, 2014)
25. Y. Ma, T. Dey, J.M. Smith, N. Wilder, A. Mockus, Crowdsourcing the discovery of software repositories in an educational environment. *PeerJ Preprints*, 4:e2551v1
26. R.P. McDonald, *Factor Analysis and Related Methods* (Psychology Press, London, 2014)
27. A. Mockus. Large-scale code reuse in open source software, in *ICSE'07 International Workshop on Emerging Trends in FLOSS Research and Development*, Minneapolis, Minnesota, 21 May 2007
28. A. Mockus, Amassing and indexing a large sample of version control systems: towards the census of public source code history, in *6th IEEE Working Conference on Mining Software Repositories*, 16–17 May 2009
29. A. Mockus, Succession: measuring transfer of code and developer productivity, in *2009 International Conference on Software Engineering*, ACM Press, Vancouver, CA, 12–22 May 2009
30. A. Mockus, Organizational volatility and its effects on software defects, in *ACM SIGSOFT/FSE*, Santa Fe, New Mexico, 7–11 November 2010, pp. 117–126
31. A. Mockus, Engineering big data solutions, in *ICSE'14 FOSE*, 2014, pp. 85–99
32. A. Mockus, J. Herbsleb, Expertise browser: a quantitative approach to identifying expertise, in *2002 International Conference on Software Engineering*, ACM Press, Orlando, Florida, 19–25 May 2002, pp. 503–512
33. S. Mousavi, T. Zhou, C, Tian, Delayed parity generation in mds storage codes, in *2018 IEEE International Symposium on Information Theory (ISIT)* (IEEE, 2018), pp. 1889–1893
34. N. Nagappan, B. Murphy, V.R. Basili, The influence of organizational structure on software quality: an empirical case study, in *ICSE 2008*, 2008, pp. 521–530
35. J. Pearl, Bayesian networks. *Department of Statistics, UCLA*, 2011
36. K.V. Rashmi, N.S. Shah, P. Vijay Kumar, Optimal exact-regenerating codes for distributed storage at the MSR and MBR points via a product-matrix construction. IEEE Trans. Inf. Theory **57**(8), 5227–5239 (2011)
37. B. Ray, D. Posnett, V. Filkov, P. Devanbu, A large scale study of programming languages and code quality in Github, in *Proceedings of the 22nd ACM SIGSOFT International Symposium on Foundations of Software Engineering* (ACM, 2014), pp. 155–165
38. P. Rigby, Y.C. Zhu, S.M. Donadelli, A. Mockus, Quantifying and mitigating turnover-induced knowledge loss: case studies of chrome and a project at avaya, in *ICSE'16* (ACM, Austin, Texas, 2016), pp. 1006–1016
39. A. Sæbjørnsen, J. Willcock, T. Panas, D. Quinlan, Z. Su, Detecting code clones in binary executables, in *Proceedings of the Eighteenth International Symposium on Software Testing and Analysis* (ACM, 2009), pp. 117–128
40. S. Sarawagi, A. Bhamidipaty, Interactive deduplication using active learning, in *Proceedings of the Eighth ACM SIGKDD International Conference on Knowledge Discovery and Data Mining, KDD '02* (ACM, New York, NY, USA, 2002), pp. 269–278
41. M. Sariyar, A. Borg, The recordlinkage package: detecting errors in data. R J. **2**(1), 61–67 (2010)
42. M. Scutari, Learning bayesian networks in r, an example in systems biology (2013), http://www.bnlearn.com/about/slides/slides-useRconf13.pdf
43. G. Silvestri, J. Yang, A. Bozzon, A. Tagarelli, Linking accounts across social networks: the case of stackoverflow, github and twitter, in *International Workshop on Knowledge Discovery on the Web*, 2015, pp. 41–52

44. S.L. Ventura, R. Nugent, E.R.H. Fuchs, Seeing the non-starts: (some) sources of bias in past disambiguation approaches and a new public tool leveraging labeled records. Res. Policy **44**(9), 1672–1701 (2015)
45. R. Vlas, W. Robinson, C. Vlas, Evolutionary software requirements factors and their effect on open source project attractiveness, 2017
46. S.B. Wicker, V.K. Bhargava, *Reed-Solomon Codes and their Applications* (Wiley, New Jersey, 1999)
47. W.E. Winkler, Overview of record linkage and current research directions. Technical report, Bureau of the census, 2006
48. Q. Zheng, A. Mockus, M. Zhou, A method to identify and correct problematic software activity data: exploiting capacity constraints and data redundancies, in *ESEC/FSE'15* (ACM, Bergamo, Italy, 2015), pp. 637–648
49. M. Zhou, A. Mockus, Developer fluency: achieving true mastery in software projects, in *ACM SIGSOFT/FSE*, Santa Fe, New Mexico, 7–11 November 2010, pp. 137–146
50. J. Zhu, M. Zhou, A. Mockus, The relationship between folder use and the number of forks: a case study on github repositories, in *ESEM*, Torino, Italy, 2014, pp. 30:1–30:4

Chapter 2
Mining Data to Profile Communication in FLOSS Communities

Barbara Russo, Juergen Tragust and Xiaofeng Wang

Abstract FLOSS projects generate big data of different types, produced throughout the development process, which is a valuable source of information on the process, product, and the organization of FLOSS projects. However, the information such data carries may sometimes be incomplete or become soon obsolete. To exemplify the potential and the limits of mining data from FLOSS projects, this chapter presents a study on how to mine social media data from an open-source community (e.g., how to reconstruct conversation of several developers), to make sense of their communication structure (e.g., use measures of social network analysis to model developers' communication), and surface the social networks that matter but are hidden underneath the large amount of data (e.g., unveil developers' roles and competencies). In the study, twitter data related to the Drupal Core project was mined, including both data on developer twitter accounts as well as tweets from these accounts. Online conversations among the Drupal Core developers were reconstructed from the mined data, and analyzed using both descriptive statistics and social network analysis. Our study demonstrates a concrete approach of investigating and surfacing hidden social networks that really matter to an open-source community, which may lead to the improvement of online communication practices used by the community.

2.1 Data Produced by FLOSS Ecosystems

FLOSS projects generate big data of different types (e.g., social media) produced all through the development process. Such data is a valuable source of information on the process, product, and the organization of FLOSS projects. The information it carries can be exploited to describe or predict properties of a FLOSS project and its ecosystem.

Unfortunately, the information such data carries may sometimes be incomplete or become soon obsolete.

B. Russo (✉) · J. Tragust · X. Wang
Free University of Bozen, Bolzano, Italy
e-mail: Barbara.Russo@unibz.it

© Springer Nature Singapore Pte Ltd. 2019
B. Fitzgerald et al. (eds.), *Towards Engineering Free/Libre Open Source Software (FLOSS) Ecosystems for Impact and Sustainability*,
https://doi.org/10.1007/978-981-13-7099-1_2

Incomplete data may be due to unobservable or unaccessible phenomenon for the specific project. For example, not all data in developers' chats can be publicly accessible [1]. And obsolescence of data may be caused by fast evolution of practices, technologies, or development needs in a FLOSS project.

Projects developed within FLOSS ecosystems have a great advantage in this respect. Partial data of a specific FLOSS project may be completed or gathered from other projects of the same ecosystem and then used to build tools and support practices for the benefit of all projects in the ecosystem. For example, data stored in code repositories can be exploited to recommend developers in their tasks (e.g., [2]).

To exemplify the potential and the limits of mining data from FLOSS ecosystems, this chapter illustrates a study on how to mine social media data from an open-source community (e.g., how to reconstruct conversation of several developers), make sense of their communication structure (e.g., use measures of social analysis to model developers' communication), and surface the social networks that matter but are hidden underneath the large amount of data (e.g., unveil developers' roles and competencies).

2.2 Unveil Social Networks that Matter: An Analysis of the Twitter Conversations Among Drupal Core Developers

2.2.1 Background and Related Work

Effective communication is a key success factor for open-source software development communities. Given the distributed nature of these communities, online communication channels play a key role in the communication of community members, which in turn impact software development activities. One of the important social media venues where communication happens is Twitter. Launched in 2006, Twitter has become more and more popular over the years. Researchers from different fields have been investigating the Twitter phenomenon. The social and public nature of Twitter resonates well with the open nature of FLOSS communities.

The early studies of Twitter find that, apart from information sharing and news notification, interaction is also an important aspect of Twitter usage. The majority of the studies of interaction on Twitter focus on the "following" relationship of Twitter, such as [3]. However, as Huberman et al. [4] argue, the linked structures of social networks do not reveal actual interactions among people. While the standard definition of a social network embodies the notion of all the people with whom one shares a social relationship, in reality people interact with very few of those listed as part of their network. One important reason behind this fact is that attention is a scarce resource in the age of the web. Scarcity of attention and the daily rhythms of life and work make people default to interacting only with those interested users.

One type of interactions that may reveal the social network that matters to community members is conversation on Twitter. Java et al. [5] in their study back in 2007 already show that conversation is a major user intention on Twitter, in addition to information sharing and news notification. Actually in the early days since there was no direct way for people to comment or reply to their friends' tweets, early adopters started using the "@" symbol followed by a username for replies. Twitter officially added "@reply" in 2010. Honey and Herring [6] examine Twitter communications focusing especially on the role attached to the "@" sign, and discover that most conversations are built up of three to five messages involving two people with obtaining responses in less than 30 minutes. In the work of Bruns [7], public Twitter conversations concerning a specific #hashtag were retrieved first. Then, the @reply tweets were further extracted. After all @replies were extracted from the whole data, a simplistic social network was constructed to visualize the @reply network existing between participating users. The author remarks that this work serves further more detailed studies in the visualization of @reply tweets in Twitter #hashtag communities.

Ritter et al. [8] establish in their paper an approach to modeling dialog acts. The authors have examined an amount of 1.3 million Twitter conversations taken from the Twitter public timeline, and applied a filter on posts without a reply tweet and on non-English conversations. They built two models to discover dialog acts in an unsupervised manner—a conversational model, and a conversation and topic model. In another work, based on about 40 million reply tweet pairs posted to Twitter between September 2008 and February 2009, Bliss et al. [9] construct and examine the revealed social network structure from the reciprocal reply tweets and dynamics over the time scales of days, weeks, and months. Their particular focus is to investigate patterns of sentiment expression in these reply tweets. The data they collected was from general Twitter users that they had access to during the given study period, not from a specific community. The study used the social network analysis approach to construct the social networks based on the reply tweets. It looked at the pairs of reply tweets that were reciprocal (which means the two Twitter users replied to each other through tweets) and built the directed network of Twitter users using these pairs.

In brief, the conversational aspect of Twitter is not sufficiently studied, let alone in the open-source software development context. This is the knowledge gap that our work intends to fill up. Before we present our approach to analyze Twitter conversations among open-source community members, we need to briefly introduce the key social network analysis concepts relevant to this study.

2.2.2 Social Network Analysis and Key Concepts

A social network is a network of relationships, which connects social actors such as individuals or organizations. This social network can be used to investigate the structure of whole social entities. To study such networks, social network analysis is used. The key concepts from social network analysis that are relevant to this study come from the following three main categories:

1. Network cohesion—characterization of a network's structure. It includes the following key parameters:

   Reciprocity   Can be calculated only in directed graphs. It is the number of relations which are reciprocated (i.e., there is an edge in both directions) divided by the total number of relations in the network.

   Network density   A network's density is the ratio of the number of edges in the network over the total number of possible edges between all pairs of nodes. Through this value, the connection of the network can be revealed.

   Network clustering coefficient   A node's clustering coefficient is the density of its neighborhood (i.e., the network consisting only of this node and all other nodes directly connected to it).

   Diameter/Average distance   The longest shortest path (distance) between any two nodes in a network is called the network's diameter. It indicates how long it will take at most to reach any node in the network (sparser networks will generally have greater diameters). The average of all shortest paths in a network is also interesting because it indicates how far apart any two nodes will be on average (average distance).

2. Key players—who are the key/central nodes in the network. It includes the following key parameters:

   Degree centrality/In-degree centrality/Out-degree centrality   The in- or out-degree of a node is the number of links that lead into or out of the node. Useful in assessing which nodes are central.

   Closeness centrality   The mean length of all shortest paths from a node to all other nodes in the network (i.e., how many hops on average it takes to reach every other node).

   Betweenness centrality   The number of shortest paths that pass through a node divided by all shortest paths in the network.

   Eigenvector centrality   A node's eigenvector centrality is proportional to the sum of the eigenvector centralities of all nodes directly connected to it. (This is similar to how Google ranks web pages: links from highly linked to pages count more).

3. Tie Strength—adding weights to edges helps to identify strong or weak ties in a network.

2.2.3   Research Approach

The open-source community chosen to be studied is the Drupal community. Drupal is one popular open-source content management system (CMS) which powers more than 1 million websites and the engine behind 12% of the web's top 100,000 most trafficked websites which use a CMS. Drupal has more than 15 years of history. The community involves more than 35,000 globally distributed developers (by the time of the data collection in April 2014). Twitter has been used both by the community collectively and by the developers individually since 2007. This makes the Drupal community an appropriate case to study. More specifically, we focus on the Drupal Core Project. In the Drupal community, the term "core" means anything outside of the "sites" folder of a Drupal installation. It is the stock element of Drupal. This focus allows us to draw a boundary of the study due to the large amount of data that needed to be dealt with.

2.2.3.1 Data Collection Process

The main data collection activity required by this study is to collect Twitter conversations among Drupal Core developers. Figure 2.1 illustrates the data collection process. It can be divided into two major steps: (1) tweets trawling and (2) conversation reconstructing.

Tweets Trawling The first step of tweets trawling was to obtain the list of Twitter accounts that belong to the contributors of the Drupal Core project. We found the list of Drupal Core contributors on the Drupal website in which all the committers were listed. The number of committers retrieved at the time of our study (April 2014) was 93. The retrieval of their Twitter accounts included the following action points:

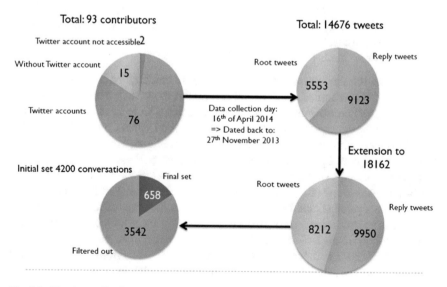

Fig. 2.1 The data collection process

1. At the same webpage where we obtained the list of Drupal Core committers, each committer's Drupal name is a link to his or her Drupal profile page. Many developers include their Twitter account information in the "Twitter url" field.
2. If the field is empty in the profile page of a developer, his Drupal name or IRC (Internet Relay Chat) nickname will be used as a search keyword on Twitter website. If such a Twitter account with Drupal name exists, the description of the account and timeline tweets will be further inspected to make sure that the account owner is a Drupal Core developer, using personal information listed in the profile as references, e.g., full name, gender, country, Linkedin profile.
3. If the search with a Drupal name does not yield any result, we use the full name (whenever it is available on the profile) as the search keyword and repeat the same inspection process described in Step 2 to decide if the Twitter account belongs to a Drupal Core developer.

As the result, we have retrieved 78 Twitter accounts that belong to 78 Drupal Core developers.

The second step was to retrieve the data about these Twitter accounts, including the user name of a Twitter account, the description of the account given by the user, the geographic location of the user, the date when the account was created, the number of followers, the number of followees, and the number of tweets.

The third step was to retrieve all the tweets from these accounts. The number of contributor Twitter accounts was reduced to 76 after this step, since one developer has 0 tweet, and the other set the profile private thus did not allow public access to its tweets.

In order to retrieve all data in a batch mode, we used the twitteR package via the statistical data-mining tool R (www.r-project.org) to interact with Twitter API. At the time of our study, the Twitter API limits the number of retrieved tweets to 3,200 maximum per account.

Conversation Reconstructing To rebuild the structures of the conversations from the retrieved tweets turned out to be not as straightforward as we wished. Since our study focus was on the interactions among the Drupal Core contributors, we were interested in the conversations that involve at least two Drupal Core contributors. To be able to reconstruct the conversations correctly, we needed to have all the tweets from all the 76 developers to start with. This could not be done for the whole period that these developers started using Twitter. Since all the tweets were dated back from the data collection day (16-04-2014), we decided the time range of the conversations that we investigated should be between the shortest timeline we retrieved from the Drupal Core contributors, to be sure the tweets from all the developers are considered within the time frame. Based on this observation, we identified the time range from November 27, 2013 to April 16, 2014. The number of tweets from the Drupal Core developers that fall in this time range is 14,676 among which the tweets that are reply to other tweets count 9,123, around 62.2% of the collected tweets.

The tweets from Drupal Core developers alone are not sufficient. In a conversation that involves the community members, the users who are not from the same community may also be involved, due to the public nature of Twitter. If the tweets from these noncommunity members are on the path of a conversational branch or as the head of a conversation that involves the community members, they need to be retrieved in order to properly reconstruct this branch or the conversation. The tweets that we should retrieve are those that are in the paths or the heads of the conversations. After this step, the number of tweets expanded to 18,162, among which the reply tweets are increased to 9,950.

After we have collected all the needed tweets in one place, we reconstructed the conversations in a top-down manner, starting from the head tweet (a tweet that has replies but is not a reply to another tweet), using R scripts we programmed. Initially, we have reconstructed 4200 conversations. After excluding those that only one Drupal developer is involved, we obtained a final set of 658 conversations that satisfy the condition of including at least two Drupal Core developers. This set of conversations is taken to the data analysis step.

One point worth noting is that most reconstructed conversations are partial of the whole conversations. A conversation can have more than one branch at any level. If the branch does not involve any Drupal Core developer that branch is not reconstructed using our approach, because we have no way to know who are those non-Drupal developers involved, and the information on a tweet provided by Twitter API does not allow to identify the downstream tweets, only upstream ones. For this reason, a reconstructed conversation tree using our approach can be only a part of a whole conversation that happens on Twitter. However, due to the focus of the approach is to investigate the conversations happening among community members, this partiality is not an issue.

2.2.3.2 Data Analysis Process

The analysis of the Twitter conversations is also divided into two main steps: (1) describing Twitter conversations and (2) constructing and analyzing social networks based on Twitter conversations.

Describing Twitter Conversations There are certain attributes of a conversation that can be defined and the values of which should be captured, to have a proper overview of the conversations happening on Twitter.

We proposed the following attributes:

- The number of tweets in a conversation.
- The number of users involved in a conversation.
- The number of team members involved in a conversation.
- The depth of a conversation, which is defined as the longest branch of the tree.
- The starting time of a conversation.
- The duration of a conversation.
- The category of a conversation, which can be

  - general, which is not directed to anyone;

– direct public, which is directed to a specific person but can be seen by all the followers of the initiating person; and
– direct private, which is directed to a specific person and only can be seen by the followers who also follow that person.

• The initiator of the conversation, which can be either a team member or a person outside the team.

Constructing and Analyzing Social Networks based on Twitter Conversation, and conduct further analysis of the formed social networks, to better understand the dynamic interactions among the Drupal Core developers via Twitter. We constructed the following two social networks drawing upon the conversations:

– Weighted, undirected network: We linked two contributors if they were involved in at least one conversation, even though they may not directly converse using "@reply". The weight of their linkage is decided by the number of same conversations they were involved.
– Weighted, directed network: We linked two contributors if only they have directly conversed via tweets using "@reply". In this case, the linkage is directional from the contributor who replied to the one whose tweet was being replied to. The weight of their linkage is decided by the times that this direct reply happens. Note that in this case, the linkage between two contributors can be bidirectional; however, each direction has its own weight.

To make better sense of the two social networks, we also constructed the third social network based on the following relationship between the developers. The following relationship is the basis upon which the conversations can happen, and therefore it serves as a baseline to compare the two social networks drawing upon the conversations. The social network based on the following relationship is unweighted because the following relationship does not bear any weight. However, it is directional from the contributor who follows to the one who is being followed. The following relationship can be reciprocal which means that the two contributors follow each other.

The social network attributes that are meaningful to examine for the three social networks including the measurements of network cohesion (reciprocity, network density, network diameter and average distance, and average coefficient), and the key players (degree, closeness, betweenness as well as eigenvector centrality). Table 2.1 shows what these concepts can mean in terms of the constructed social networks.

Gephi is the main tool we used to analyze the three social networks and obtain the values of the listed properties. Since Gephi does not provide functions to calculate reciprocity, we used UCINET to obtain the reciprocity values of the three networks.

At the end of this step, we also compared the roles of the Drupal Core developers played in these social networks to the roles they played in the development in terms of their commits to the project.

Table 2.1 Interpretation of social network analysis concepts in terms of twitter conversations

Social network properties	Weighted, nondirected conversation network	Weighted, directed conversation network	Unweighted, directed following network
Reciprocity	(not applicable)	The ratio of bidirectional conversations over the total direct conversations	The ratio of reciprocal following relationships among all following relationships
Network density	How often developers are involved in the same conversations	How often developers directly converse with each other	How often developers are following one another
Network clustering coefficient	Existence of subgroups of developers who converse together	Existence of subgroups of developers who directly converse	Existence of subgroups of developers who follow each other
Diameter/Average distance	The maximal/average steps needed for two developers to be in the same conversation	The maximal/average steps needed for two developers to have a direct conversation	The maximal/Average steps needed for two developers to follow one another
Degree centrality/In-degree centrality/Out-degree centrality	The number of developers with whom a given developer is involved in the same conversations	In-degree centrality: the number of developers that directly reply to a given developer Out-degree centrality: the number of developers that a given developer directly replies to	In-degree centrality: the number of developers that follow a given developer Out-degree centrality: the number of developers that a given developer follows
Closeness centrality	How fast a developer can involve everyone else in a conversation	How fast a developer can have a direct conversation with everyone else	How fast a developer can have a following relationship with everyone else
Betweenness centrality	How likely a developer is the bridge for two other developers to have a conversation	How likely a developer is the bridge for two other developers to have a direct conversation	How likely a developer is the bridge for two other developers to have a following relation
Eigenvector centrality	How well a developer interacts with the other active developers in terms of conversation	How well a developer directly converse with the other active developers in terms of direct conversation	How well a developer follows/is followed by other well following/followed developers
Tie strength	Which pairs are most often involved in the same conversations	Which pairs are most often converse directly	(not applicable)

2.2.4   Unveil the Social Networks that Matter

Observations on the 78 Twitter Accounts of the Drupal Core Users
The Drupal Core developers are distributed mainly in America and Europe. Among the 78 Twitter accounts studied, the earliest one was opened on October 7, 2006, and the latest was on June 8, 2013. The majority of the accounts were opened in 2008 and 2009, as shown in Fig. 2.2.

The conversational tweets from the Drupal Core developers during the studied period are 9,123, about 62.2% of the total tweets they tweeted during the same period. This shows that Twitter is heavily used for the conversational purpose by the Drupal Core developers. The number of conversations by month is shown in Fig. 2.3. It can be seen that the number of conversations happening over the time does not vary a lot. 619 out of 658 conversations started as public and to general audience. In comparison, very few conversations (39) started by addressing a specific Twitter user directly. Among these direct conversations, 34 are private and 5 are intended to be heard by a wider audience. Table 2.2 shows the descriptive statistics of the conversations that Drupal developers have on Twitter in terms of number of people involved, number of tweets, and duration of the conversations.

Fig. 2.2 Twitter accounts opening per year

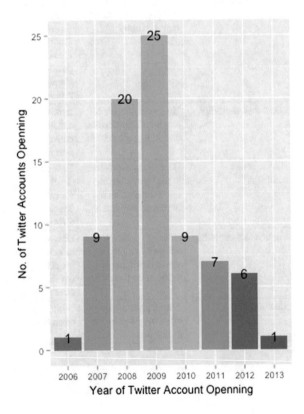

Fig. 2.3 Number of
conversations per month

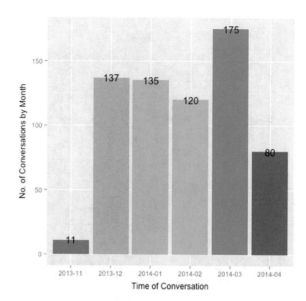

Table 2.2 Descriptive statistics of the studied conversations

Statistics	NoT	Depth	NoU	NoDC	Duration
min	2	2	2	2	24
max	53	42	10	6	2664440
range	51	40	8	4	2664416
median	4	3	3	2	6475.5
mean	5.45	4.07	3.18	2.29	41605.70
std.dev	5.09	3.24	1.31	0.68	189073.56

It can be seen based on the statistics reported in Table 2.2 that the majority of the conversations involving the Drupal Core developers are short in terms of both the Number of Tweets and Duration. The mean of NoT is 5.45, and most often there are only two tweets exchanged. The mean of the Duration is 6475.5 s (less than two hours). Meanwhile, the mean of the Depth of the conversations is 4.07. The majority of them have Depth of 2 only. This can mean that the conversations on Twitter are mainly quick chats. However, it is noticeable that there are some exceptions. The longest conversation has in total 53 tweets, the depth of which is 33. It involves six Twitter users, among them two Drupal Core developers. The conversation lasted more than 20 hours. The topic of the conversation is not related to the Drupal Core project, but general discussion on free speech. In contrast, the deepest conversation has 42 levels. It is also the second longest conversation and includes 52 tweets in total. Seven Twitter users including 3 Drupal Core developers were involved. It went on for more than 23 hours. Similarly, the topic is general about the differences in cultures.

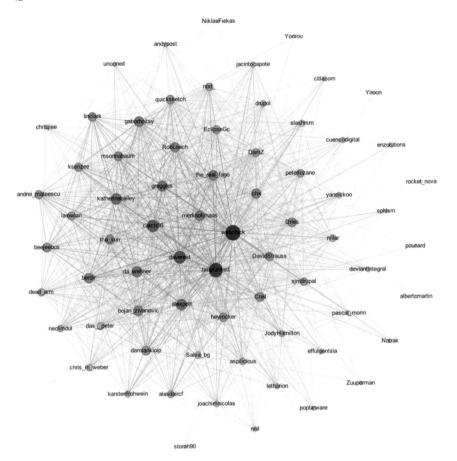

Fig. 2.4 Social network formed by following relationship

Table 2.2 also shows that the conversations are mainly dialogs since most often only two Drupal Core Developers were involved. The largest number of Drupal Core Developers involved in a conversation is 6, while 10 is the largest number of Twitter users involved in one conversation. We inspected the six conversations that involved the most Drupal Core developers. Two of them are related to Drupal Core project or software development, the rest are all social in nature, either about marriage, or being a parent. However, these are the social chatters somehow related to the community. The two conversations that involved most Twitter users (10) however have only 2 Drupal Core developers involved, respectively, and therefore these seem the interactions in a wider social context.

Figure 2.4 shows the following network as a comparison to the two networks that were constructed based on the studied conversations, which are shown in Figs. 2.5 and 2.6, one is weighted, undirected network while the other is weighted, directed. The nodes of larger size and darker color are the ones that have more links and located

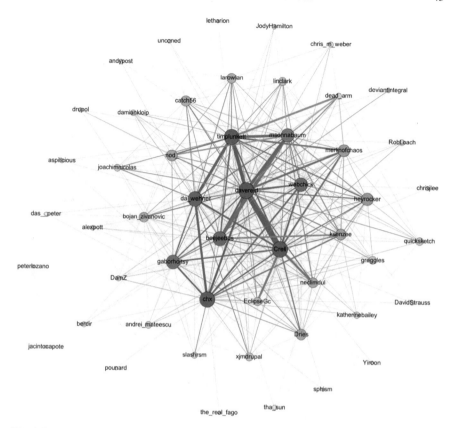

Fig. 2.5 Social network formed by conversations that Drupal Core developers are involved in

in the center of the diagrams. Since the following relationship is the basis for which conversations happen, the two conversation networks actually highlight the linkages in the following network through which more active interactions happen. It can be seen that the nodes in the center of following relationship are also in the center of the two conversation networks, even though the exact sizes and shades of these nodes change across the diagrams.

A more accurate comparison of the three networks in terms of relevant network properties is shown in Table 2.3. The number of nodes that are involved in the conversations we examined is 51, 65.38% of those who have Twitter accounts. 48 developers have directly talked to one another using "@reply" of Twitter feature during the period we have studied. In average, a developer has been involved in the same conversations with more than eight other developers. The average frequency of being involved in conversations with the same developer is higher than three. In contrast, the average number of directly conversed developers is less than five. The average frequency of directly interacting with the same developer is nearly three.

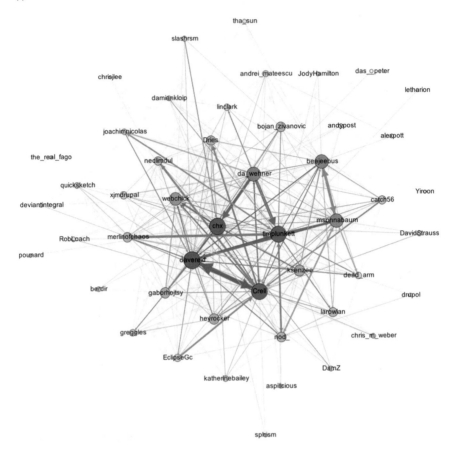

Fig. 2.6 Social Network formed by direct Conversations among Drupal Core Developers

In comparison to the dense following network (network density equals to 0.23), the two conversation networks are sparser (0.11 and 0.06, respectively). This is consistent with what visually shows in Figs. 2.5 and 2.6. This means that the following relationship is a better connected network than the two conversation networks.

However, it is surprising to see that the reciprocity of the direct conversation network is higher than that of the following network, both dyad based and edgewise. It means that the developers more often reciprocate a reply tweet that addresses to him or her than reciprocate a following action from other developers. The three networks have similar diameter value (3 and 4), which means that it takes at most 3 or 4 steps from one node to any other nodes in the network. Therefore, even though the two conversation networks are sparser than the following network in terms of number of edges and average degrees. They are equally dense in terms of reachability between nodes. Similarly, the values of the average path length of the three networks are close too, as shown in Table 2.3.

Table 2.3 The property values of the three social networks under the study

Network Properties	Weighted, nondirected conversation network	Weighted, directed conversation network	Unweighted, directed following network
Number (percentage) of nodes connected	51 (65.38%)	48 (61.54%)	70 (89.74%)
Number of edges	333	369	1365
Average degree	8.54	4.73	17.5
Average weighted degree	29.26	14.04	—
Network density	0.11	0.06	0.23
Reciprocity	—	0.53 (Dyad-based)/0.69 (Arc-based)	0.34 (Dyad-based)/0.51 (Arc-based)
Network diameter	3	4	4
Average path length	1.80	2.10	1.78
Average clustering coefficient	0.78	0.49	0.45

In addition, the average clustering coefficient of weighted undirected network indicates that the same subgroup of developers tends to be involved in the same conversations. Given the relatively high average clustering coefficient and the short average path length, the undirected conversation network might have the properties of a small world. In comparison, the tendency of direct conversation with the same subgroup of developers is not as obvious. It is more evenly spread out, similar to the following relationship.

We also closely examined the key players in the three networks in terms of degree centrality, closeness centrality, betweenness centrality, eigenvector centrality, and tie strength. A similar set of developers appear as the key players in conversations in terms of the number of developers they interact through conversations (degree centrality), their closeness to all other developers, their potential bridging roles between subgroup of developers, and how well they interact with other people who are also active in conversations. The same pattern can be observed also in the key players of the following network, even though they are slightly different set of developers in contrast to those of conversation networks.

We also examined the Drupal profiles of the key players in these networks in terms of their activity and contribution to the Drupal Core project and overall Drupal community. It turned out that they are also core developers and top code committers in the community. The developers who appear to be at the peripheral of the development are also not active in the conversations with other developers on Twitter. There are just very few exceptions that developers are active in one arena but barely visible in the other.

2.3   Conclusion

The study presented in this chapter investigated conversations of open-source software developers on Twitter and as a special case the Drupal Core project, as an example of mining social media data to surface hidden communication structures in FLOSS communities. Twitter was launched in 2006 and has become more and more popular over the years. The general user intention consists of conversing, sharing information, and news awareness. Because of its popularity and growing community, many researchers have investigated in the Twitter phenomenon. These studies vary in nature, from the usage of Twitter in software development communities to the social network analysis and reconstructing @reply conversations. However, the conversational aspect of Twitter in an open-source software development context is not sufficiently studied. This study attempted to provide an approach to enable a better understanding of how communication happens within an open-source software development community, and as a special case the Drupal Core Project.

Following the research approach presented in the chapter, researchers and practitioners, in both open-source and commercial area, can investigate and surface hidden social networks that really matter to a community, and improve the communication practices used by the community based on what can be learned through analyzing these communication structures and contents. For example, the future work can conduct content analysis to get a more qualitative understanding of what issues they actually converse about. In addtion, our study looked at a very small time range. Having an extended data collection, consisting of a longer time period, would lead to a more detailed result. Also, longitudinal studies of the evolution of conversation networks can be conducted, to understand if and how the communication behaviors and habits of developers change over the time. Last but now least, since the whole process of the data collection, reconstruction of the conversations, and the building of the social networks was highly manual and took a lot of effort, it would be a welcomed improvement if the process could be automated. In our study, we used TwitteR, Gephi, and UCINET; however, it would be intriguing to see how this approach could be expanded by using other tools that allow automation.

References

1. L. Zou, W.W. Song, Lda-tm: A two-step approach to twitter topic data clustering, in *2016 IEEE International Conference on Cloud Computing and Big Data Analysis (ICCCBDA)* (2016), pp. 342–347
2. L. Villarroel, G. Bavota, B. Russo, R. Oliveto, M.D. Penta, Release planning of mobile apps based on user reviews, in *Proceedings of the 38th International Conference on Software Engineering, ICSE 2016*, Austin, TX, USA, 14–22 May (2016), pp. 14–24, http://doi.acm.org/10.1145/2884781.2884818
3. E. Baumer, A. Leis, Minimalists and Zealots: Genres of participation in following on Twitter, in *CHI 2010 Workshop on Microblogging: What and How Can We Learn From It?* (2010)

4. B.A. Huberman, D.M. Romero, F. Wu, Social networks that matter: Twitter under the micro-scope. SSRN Electron. J. (2008), http://ssrn.com/paper=1313405
5. A. Java, X. Song, T. Finin, B. Tseng, Why we Twitter: understanding the microblogging effect in user intentions and communities, in *Joint 9th WEBKDD and 1st SNA-KDDWorkshop 07* (2007), http://workshops.socialnetworkanalysis.info/websnakdd2007/papers/submission_21.pdf
6. C. Honeycutt, S.C. Herring, Beyond microblogging: conversation and collaboration via Twitter, in *Proceedings of the 42nd Annual Hawaii International Conference on System Sciences, HICSS* (2009)
7. A. Bruns, How long is a tweet? mapping dynamic conversation networks on twitter using Gawk and Gephi. Inf. Commun. Soc. **15**(9), 1323–1351 (2012)
8. A. Ritter, C. Cherry, B. Dolan, Unsupervised modeling of twitter conversations, *The 2010 Annual Conference of the North American Chapter of the Association for Computational Linguistics* (2010), pp. 172–180, http://nparc.cisti-icist.nrc-cnrc.gc.ca/npsi/ctrl?action=rtdoc& an=16885300, http://dl.acm.org/citation.cfm?id=1858019
9. C.A. Bliss, I.M. Kloumann, K.D. Harris, C.M. Danforth, P.S. Dodds, Twitter reciprocal reply networks exhibit assortativity with respect to happiness. J. Comput. Sci. **3**(5), 388–397 (2012)

Chapter 3
A Preliminary Theory for Open-Source Ecosystem Microeconomics

Nicolas Jullien, Klaas-Jan Stol and James D. Herbsleb

Abstract While there has been substantial empirical work identifying factors that influence the contribution to, and use of open-source software, we have as yet little theory that identifies the key constructs and relationships that would allow us to explain and predict how open-source ecosystems function. The absence of ecosystem theory is particularly alarming as open-source software works its way more broadly and deeply into the economy. The problem facing policymakers is how to provide support and resources when needed, without distorting decision-making, demotivating volunteers, serving special interests at the expense of others, and maintaining the communities that take on and guide the work. What is needed is a clearly articulated and empirically validated theory of open-source ecosystems. This chapter provides a sketch of such a theory in the form of a set of propositions, which may form the foundation for future empirical work.

3.1 Introduction

Markets play a key organizing role in most economic systems. Understanding how markets work is critical for effective economic policy. It identifies the levers that policymakers can manipulate to achieve desired effects. Microeconomics uses constructs such as supply and demand, allocation of resources, and equilibria to build

N. Jullien (✉)
LEGO-M@rsouin, IMT Atlantique, Brest, France
e-mail: Nicolas.Jullien@imt-atlantique.fr

K.-J. Stol
Lero—the Irish Software Research Centre, School of Computer Science and Information Technology, University College Cork, Cork, Republic of Ireland
e-mail: k.stol@cs.ucc.ie

J. D. Herbsleb
Institute for Software Research, School of Computer Science, Carnegie Mellon University, Pittsburgh, PA, USA
e-mail: jdh@cs.cmu.edu

© Springer Nature Singapore Pte Ltd. 2019
B. Fitzgerald et al. (eds.), *Towards Engineering Free/Libre Open Source Software (FLOSS) Ecosystems for Impact and Sustainability*,
https://doi.org/10.1007/978-981-13-7099-1_3

models that explain and predict key phenomena such as price setting and the flow of resources to various producers. It allows policymakers to identify market failures, identify abuse of monopoly positions, and other undesirable phenomena and provides a theory that points to policy decisions that can have a beneficial impact, minimizing harmful side effects that result in suboptimal outcomes.

Open-source ecosystems perform functions analogous to those performed by markets, but they do so without price signals, revenue streams, monetary returns, or other key theoretical mechanisms that are the stock in trade of economists modeling markets. While there has been substantial empirical work identifying factors that influence the contribution to, and use of open-source software [17], we have as yet little theory that identifies the key constructs and relationships that would allow us to explain and predict how open-source ecosystems function.

The absence of ecosystem theory is particularly alarming as open-source software works its way more broadly and deeply into the economy. As pointed out in a recent report by Eghbal [18], open-source ecosystems are becoming critical digital infrastructure underpinning the publicly and privately produced computational resources we rely on. And it is increasingly apparent that this infrastructure is often neglected and under-resourced, with negative consequences ranging from slowed product development to critical security flaws[1] and propagation of defects and version incompatibilities.

The problem facing policymakers is how to provide support and resources when needed, without distorting decision-making, demotivating volunteers, serving special interests at the expense of others, and maintaining the communities that take on and guide the work. Inappropriate application of resources, for example, could extend the life of a project that should be allowed to decline and be replaced. Adding paid developers to a project could demotivate other volunteers, and reduce the intrinsic motivation of those who are compensated, reducing future contributions. If support is provided to move in a particular technical direction, it could give rise to conflict and potential fragmentation of the community. Interventions that do not respect the logic and underlying principles and relationships of open-source ecosystems could easily cause more harm than good, and weaken the very ecosystems it is designed to help.

What is needed is a clearly articulated and empirically validated theory of open-source ecosystems. Such a theory should:

- Explain why, how, and when key resources—primarily the work of developers—are attracted to or depart from a project or an ecosystem.
- Explain why, how, and when projects and ecosystems move through a life cycle, from initiation, growth, maturity, and decline and death.
- Explain how decisions about use are made, and how the cumulatively influence the socio-technical position of a project within an ecosystem, and the relations of ecosystems to each other.

---

[1]For example: https://en.wikipedia.org/wiki/Heartbleed.

The remainder of this chapter provides a sketch of such a theory in the form of a set of propositions, which may form the foundation for future empirical work.

3.2   The Three Stages of an Open-Source Project

The Stanford economist Paul David identified three factors that influence growth and sustainability of FLOSS projects [16], factors, which define three phases in an open-source project life: first, projects will not be able to enter Phase 2 without achieving sufficient community commitment. In Phase 2, the rate of innovation through the addition of new features will ensure growth to Phase 3. In this phase, existential threats emerge through the problem of maintainability, which may be exacerbated by contributor fatigue as key maintainers may leave the project, leaving the project's future in jeopardy.

This three-phased idea is a familiar concept in software system development, adoption, and also in project staffing. Software development follows an S-curve process in terms of efficiency, or productivity, called the Rayleigh–Norden curve [41]. In Phase 1, investments have to be made to develop the foundations of the project, while the production of features might be slow, but the number of people may stay low. After a point, the project enters Phase 2, which is the development phase during which many features are added and the total size of the team may increase. During this phase, the level of productivity tends to be high. After some time, when most of the needs have been addressed, the project enters Phase 3, which is characterized by a decrease in the efficiency of the allocation of resources, and a need to decrease the size of the team affected to the project. Koch [32] showed that this three-phase evolution in terms of software production applies to open source as well.

As open source has traditionally been a voluntary-based movement [35], this is not a surprise either as it also echoes the analyses on people's engagement into a collective action [37, 42], or an "action taken together by a group of people whose goal is to enhance their status and achieve a common objective" (Wikipedia quoting *Encyclopædia Britannica*). As explained by Marwell and Oliver [37], motivations and engagement of participants vary, and this explains what happens in these phases in terms of involvement. The first phase attracts only those people who have a high interest in the project, and a low cost of involvement. After some point, and this is especially true for software, increasing returns to adoption start to matter, making more and more interesting to adopt the solution, and attracting new and more diverse actors [6, 15]. Finally, when the project matures, development of new functionality often slows downs and it moves into a mode that could be characterized as "maintenance," which we call Phase 3. Evidence suggests that as projects age, they struggle to recruit and retain newcomers [54]. This decrease in the growth in participants may simply be the result of, or a signal that, the project has entered a mature phase in which it needs fewer additions and thus fewer contributors [23]. Their organization is said to become increasingly bureaucratic [8]. This is not necessarily a bad thing: as Heckathorn explained (ibid), this bureaucracy makes entry more difficult (more expensive) for newcomers, and thus decrease the number of people willing to participate in such a project.

However, this can lead to the death or downfall of the project. If too many people leave too rapidly, if the project's technical or administrative structure makes it increasingly harder to integrate new features, or if, on the contrary, too many people stay for too few things to do, there is an increasing risk of conflicts and inefficient allocation of efforts. Actually, a project's decline, or "death" can occur at any phase of the project, if nobody contributes in the first phase, if growth is not properly managed in Phase 2, or, as stated above, if maturity turns into decay too soon or too quickly.

We detail the ecosystemic challenges of each phase in the remaining sections of this chapter.

3.3   Phase 1: The User-Innovator Phase

The first phase is the one which has attracted probably the most and certainly the earliest research. According to Von Hippel, beyond any motivations, the core of the incentive framework for people to get involved in the early stage of an open-source project is the "private collective" innovation model or the "user-as-innovator principle" [36, 53]: as users directly benefit from the innovation they produce, they have an incentive to produce it, and as they can expect add-on, feedback, or cumulative innovation on their own proposition, they have an incentive to freely share it. Jullien and Roudaut [29] described the difficulties to succeed for projects when the producers were not its users.

As a consequence, to evaluate the chance of success of an open-source project in Phase 1, we must focus first on incentives of individual users; developers have to get involved, and, second, the technical and organizational structures that lead them to stay. But first of all, the question is why people or organizations would initiate an open-source project.

Early-stage FLOSS projects can be classified into three categories. The first category represents the "traditional" FLOSS project, started by one or a few individuals to "scratch an itch" [43]. The causes for such itches are various: technical issues that "bother" expert programmers who decide to develop a solution, dissatisfaction with existing proposals, or a lack of existing solutions altogether. Other software solutions may be controlled by a company and lead to market inefficiency (e.g., overpriced products, too little innovation, poor user support, or poor product compatibility). A key characteristic of this type of FLOSS project is that they are solutions developed by individuals to solve a personal computing problem. Examples are widespread, with the Linux kernel perhaps the best known and most successful example. A key challenge for many of these projects is to attract a developer community—most projects have only small developer communities [11].

The second category of FLOSS projects is formerly proprietary software that has been open sourced, such as Netscape's web browser [1]. The reasons for open sourcing may vary; one reason is that a company no longer wants to spend resources on maintaining the software [52]. Another reason is to increase market share, which will also change the business model around the product (e.g., services around the product) [20, 39]. Another reason might be that a company seeks collaboration in the development of complementary assets [30]. Here again, one of the key challenges for the open sourcing company is to generate enough interest in the project that it attracts contributors.

The third category is that of the so-called "planned" FLOSS projects, typically driven by one or a consortium of companies. One well-known and recent example of this is OpenStack, which was planned by a large consortium of companies, and the goal for the companies involved is to create an industrial standard (or an industrial public good).[2] The challenges are those of the creation of an open standard, especially in the balance of the participants' incentive to support the creation of such a standard, and their interest in curving it toward their own goal. For this type of projects, the issue of raising initial investment of resources does not loom large; instead, such projects face organizational challenges such as project governance, which also characterize projects in Phase 2.

The first phase of the model presented (see Fig. 3.1 S-Curve) illustrates how successful FLOSS projects have an initial stage of growth. Whether or not a FLOSS project will attract sufficient momentum in terms of users and developers (i.e., its popularity) depends on many factors. First, projects in what we have described as Phase 1 attract only those developers who have a very strong interest in the project, or in Raymond's terms [43], those developers that share the same "itch to scratch." These developers typically face low "cost" in participating; for example, they have sufficient time to engage in the project, and they have a significant level of expertise that is required to participate in an early stage of the project when the foundations are laid out. This leads us to pose the following proposition.

Proposition 3.1 *Early-stage FLOSS projects attract developers that perceive the project to be of very high personal value (i.e., it solves a personal problem), and who have low entry barriers to participate (i.e., highly skilled, strong motivation, sufficient time to participate).*

As a FLOSS project is maturing and exhibits a basic feature set beyond the foundations of a project, the project increasingly offers value to stakeholders other than the initial developers who were simply scratching an itch. A more diverse group of stakeholders starts to become interested, including companies who may see business opportunities by leveraging the FLOSS asset for product development, or for developing services around the product. For example, Red Hat is a company (founded in 1993, two years after Linux version 0.0.1 was released) that built an extensive set of services around several very successful FLOSS projects, including the Linux

---

[2]The literature on standards is very extensive and well beyond the scope of this chapter. We refer interested readers to Swann's literature review [50].

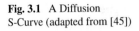

Fig. 3.1 A Diffusion
S-Curve (adapted from [45])

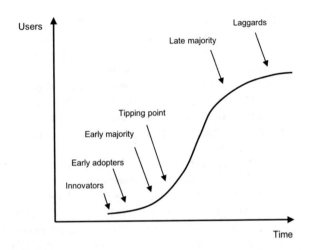

operating system and JBoss. This led Red Hat to become the first one-billion dollar open-source company in 2012, and its growth has sustained quite significantly in the years since. The process of maturation—that is, the recognition that a project has real potential—may lead to the attraction of additional developers and users, who are perhaps less skilled, or have less spare time available, but who are nevertheless highly motivated to contribute to a project that they are excited about.

Proposition 3.2 *Early-stage FLOSS projects that offer value beyond "personal interest" will attract a more diverse group of stakeholders than the initial developers.*

There is also a set of socio-technical factors that influence the attraction of new developers to a project, which is a measure of a project's popularity. In terms of technical factors, the implementation technologies may attract, but also deter developers. Modern technologies are typically perceived to be more interesting, not only due to developers' desire and interest to learn those new technologies, but also to improve future job opportunities. Projects that are based on old technologies which are no longer in favor (e.g., Fortran, COBOL) are unlikely to attract today's generation of developers who are likely more interested in modern web technologies such as JavaScript (incl. Node.js) and Python. Thus, we offer the following proposition.

Proposition 3.3 *The popularity of an early-stage FLOSS project depends on the popularity of the technology the project is written in.*

There are few analyses of why companies decide to open source one of its software since Ågerfalk and Fitzgerald [1] defined the term, as "outsourcing a formally internal software to unknown people." Companies have to adjust in order to be able to collaborate efficiently with communities beyond their organizational boundaries (see, for example, Schaarschmidt et al. [47]). Shaikh and Cornford [48] have since reaffirmed the fact that embracing an open-source strategy means embracing an open-source

Table 3.1 When outsourcing an internally produced component and how

		Central for the core business of the company?	
		Low importance	Business-critical
Potential of further evolution of the software	Low	Orphan software	Key component, software as a product or service, or internal (closed) maintenance
	High	Cooperative development software	solution, open-sourced or not depending on the strategic consequences of open sourcing the component

organization, and building trust and cooperative mechanisms with the developers. In exchange, the company, in addition to outsourcing the cost of maintaining and expanding the software can recruit competent and committed developers more easily.

However, there is still a need for a better understanding of the link between internal and external organization, and of the consequences of opening up and collaborate with potential competitors, in other words, to create a sustainable open-source ecosystem, or what we refer to here as Phase 2.

Proposition 3.4 *Projects that offer considerable potential business value will attract corporate investment if the project's value proposition is compatible with the company's strategy.*

It is worth noting, first, that not all the open-sourced software projects are aimed at creating value for companies. The traditional outsourcing strategy concerns externalizing complementary assets to specialized companies in order to decrease the total cost of ownership. (We refer to Lacity et al. [34] for a review of the literature on IT outsourcing).

If a component does not have a great potential to evolve further, it is unlikely to attract any new developers, and, if it is key for the business of the company, it is unlikely to be open-sourced [52]. If there is a potential, it is not sure that the company would want to invest its employees' time and money in developing a community. On the other hand, if a component is business critical, outsourcing may lead to too much leak toward its competitor (ibid). These simple considerations lead to Table 3.1, which summarizes the opportunity for outsourcing (and open sourcing).

Proposition 3.5 *If a software component is not critical for the core business of a company, and has a potential of evolution, the company will favor an open-source strategy to share the cost of development.*

Proposition 3.6 *If a software component is critical for the core business of a company, and has a high potential of evolution, an open-source strategy will be considered if and only if the technical structure of the software allows the company to keep some* *strategic components closed while open-sourcing the standard part to benefit from the innovative dynamic of the community.*

As appealing this analysis can be, the case of an open sourcing strategy raises many questions. For example, how can we evaluate the minimum population of skilled developers that is required for the open sourcing strategy to be considered, so as to be able to expect a community to emerge? What does a dynamic of evolution means, is being dynamic enough for a company to prevent competitors from forking and "capturing" the developer community, and the clients? How big should a population of potential clients be for this strategy to be economically sustainable? And, of course, coming back to the howto, for both the core and the complementary asset strategy, how to advertise this open-sourcing to the first contributors, in order to jump-start the ecosystem? What guarantees should a company provide, and how should it structure and publish the software source code to facilitate the entry of new developers? What is the cost of sustaining and supporting a community, and what should a company "control" themselves, and which aspects can be left to self-organizing communities, so that project management and leadership can emerge among a core of initial community developers?

To conclude this section, we can say that if the open-source licenses can be seen, in that perspective, as a new element in the companies' strategic portfolio to manage their relations with a software service provider, it would benefit from more research from fields such as strategic management and information systems regarding the parameters to take into account and the measure of these parameters in the business and financial evaluation of an open-source strategy.

If the early-stage software reaches some point of minimum viability, technically and in terms of adoption by a sufficiently large user-base, its adoption by a more general audience may start to grow. To put it in a more global framework, technology adoption, and in Roger's [45] perspective, the end of Phase 1 is characterized by going beyond the core developers team, and even to the early adopters, who if not developing directly, can give feedback, express new needs, but ask also for new support services, such as user-support mailing lists [33] to start reaching the early majority of the "simple" users.

This signals that a project has entered Phase 2, and in this "growth" stage, both the adoption rate and development efforts grow as the utility of the minimally viable product is recognized. We discuss Phase 2 next.

3.4   Phase 2: Blossoming or Fading

As adoption grows, development resources tend to flow into the project, for several distinct reasons. Volunteers are drawn by the increasing visibility and reputation-enhancing potential of contributions to the project. Companies are drawn by the high potential, but not yet fully realized, of the project for their business–at this relatively early stage, companies may be able to exert some level of control and shape the future of the project. Since the product has demonstrated its utility but is not yet feature complete, companies invest a portion of their development resources to build the functionality they need.

Proposition 3.7 *Projects that have a sound initial foundation (i.e., the project has commercial potential and represents significant value to users) will attract more developers who may have less time and skills than the original core developers, leading to an increased development velocity of the project.*

As the actors in the community diversify, their goals may diverge, too. As the project grows, the difficulty to maintain a technical coherence may also grow, as the difficulty for newcomers to contribute to the code.

How to deal with the management of stakeholders' different points of view, with the growing complexity of the code and of the organization, how to turn a technical success into a diffusion success, how to make the participation of the companies in the development economically sustainable are some of the main challenges of this phase, and will be discussed this section.

The challenge for projects at that stage is to build the governance structures, the technical infrastructure to allow each to concentrate on their own subject of interest in the project, and everybody to coordinate, so that the diverse range of interests turn into a broader project rather than a battlefield characterized by internal conflicts.

The design of the project into clearly defined modular components is key here, for economic reasons, as it facilitates and decreases the cost of producing new knowledge [4], making entry easier for a new competitor, which, as traditional standard economics pointed out, "needs only to produce a single better component, which can then hook up the market range of complementary components, than if each innovator must develop an entire system" [19]. It is also key from a software engineering [2] and organizational point of view, as it is very difficult for teams to work efficiently with too many people. In an early study of the Apache web server project, Mockus et al. [38] hypothesized that open-source projects' core teams tend to consist of no more than 15 persons, for accessibility and managerial purpose [2].

Proposition 3.8 *Sustainable open-source projects are those which succeed in (1) structuring their architecture and their organization around modules managed by small teams; (2) orchestrating the coordination of the different modules/teams.*

But what exactly characterizes a good open-source module team; which are the key qualities of good open-source contributors are questions that remain a topic of debate. Team assembly mechanisms can determine team performance [21], especially in creative teams such as those engaged in building knowledge commons (Hess and Ostrom 2006). Open-source contributor evaluation often relies on the idea of meritocracy, where developers are evaluated based on the quality and quantity of their contributions, which leads to recognition by peers [26]. However, meritocratic cultures have been demonstrated to deliver biased observations (Castilla and Bernard [10], and FLOSS communities have been specifically criticized for this shortcoming [40, 44].

Table 3.2 Relevant characteristics to identify a good open-source contributor (from [3])

	Problematic contributor	Good contributor
Communication skills (signal over noise ratio)	Too much noise/not enough information	Is good at providing the right level of information
Commitment to the project	Unmotivated/passive in seeking answers	Is motivated and does a thorough job
Working with others	Tends to find fault with others	Is generally trusting, patient with people
Pressure and stress related managing capacity	Gets nervous\stressed easily (ex.: when things do not go as expected, when there are delays or due deliverables)	Is relaxed, handles stress, technical limitations, setbacks well
Creativity	Not very creative in terms of solutions	Has an active imagination, proposes creative ideas/solutions
Quantity of code contributed	Few lines of code	An impressive quantity of code
Quality of code contributed	Tends to provide incomplete or inferior solutions	Produces efficient and well-written code, without disturbing other parts of the code
Global picture: understands the tools/technology/domain, processes behind the project	Low, does not understand beyond the talks/the modules addressed	Understands the technical and nontechnical fundamentals of the project
Documentation and testing	Does not document/test the code produced, or does so in a way not understandable by others	Documents/test well and clearly the code produced
Contribution on other aspects than code (new features, bug description)	Does not contribute beyond code production	Very active in proposing new features, tracking and documenting bugs, etc

In fact, as for other virtual teams [21], social skills in conjunction with leadership behavior affect team motivation and performance, too. Stuart and Gossin [49] demonstrated how contributors' performance is sensitive to trust and good communication within the team. And, as for any social group, Carillo et al. [9] insisted on the importance of socialization, i.e., the capacity of the open-source organization to teach the rules to newcomers, for them to become good, valuable contributors. Finally, Barcomb et al. [3], showed that even a limited number of open-source project managers may agree on the set of relevant characteristics to identify good open-source contributors, they vary in which actual characteristics they use in practice to evaluate different contributors. Even when the different managers use the same attributes, there may be disagreement on the relative importance of these attributes. (Tables 3.2, 3.3)

Table 3.3 Summary of research questions and propositions for future research on open-source ecosystems

Phase 1: Early Stage	
Research Questions	Our Propositions
How to recruit sufficient and highly skilled developers to ensure successful progress to Stage 2?	Early-stage FLOSS projects attract developers that perceive the project to be of very high personal value (i.e., it solves a personal problem), and who have low entry barriers to participate (i.e., highly skilled, strong motivation, sufficient time to participate) Early-stage FLOSS projects that offer value beyond "personal interest" will attract a more diverse group of stakeholders than the initial developers The popularity of an early-stage FLOSS project depends on the popularity of the technology the project is written in Projects that offer considerable potential business value will attract corporate investment if the project's value proposition is compatible with the company's strategy
When and how open-sourcing an in-house software component	If a software component is not critical for the core business of a company, and has a potential of evolution, the company will favor an open-source strategy to share the cost of development If a software component is critical for the core business of a company, and has a high potential of evolution, an open-source strategy will be considered if and only if the technical structure of the software allows the company to keep some strategic components closed while open-sourcing the standard part to benefit from the innovative dynamic of the community
Phase 2: Growth	
Research Questions	Our Propositions
How to design a sustainable project	Sustainable open-source projects are those which succeed in 1. Structuring their architecture and their organization around modules managed by small teams 2. Orchestrating the coordination of the different modules/teams
What is an efficient teaming and efficient management at module level as well as at project level	Team composition and skills required may vary according to 1. The technical characteristics and difficulties of the project 2. The psychological profile of the team leader If modularity and delegation of responsibility is key at the project level, the organization of this delegation and the level of centralization will vary according to 1. The technical dependencies of the modules 2. The psychological and professional profile of the project leader
Corporate investment in open-source production	The more central the role of an open-source project in a company's business (i.e., a core asset), the more a company will contribute Projects that are "stable" (i.e., little development efforts beyond basic maintenance) tend not to attract corporate investment

(continued)

Table 3.3 (continued)

Phase 1: Early Stage	
Research Questions	Our Propositions

Phase 3: Maturity and beyond	
Research Questions	Our Propositions
When does a project enter in a mature phase?	Projects that are stable in terms of number of features added/removed will lose developers over time as there is a decreasing amount of work left on the project Mature FLOSS projects tend to become more bureaucratic and rigid in terms of processes and procedures, making harder for newcomers to get involved The continuance of external perturbations leads to continued project activity, even when there is no improvement in terms of functionalities
Evolution of participation	Companies that no longer perceive a project to be of business value will stop investing in that project A project's core members are the last to leave (they are the most attached to the project), and the peripheral ones the first
Decline or death of a project	If a project becomes too bureaucratic while lacking innovation, participants may "voice," but those who resent this most are not those who have decision-making power (i.e., core members), or those with business interests (i.e., companies) If a project accepts that it has to reorganize to regain innovativeness, those who have invested the most (core members and companies) will be the most committed to participate in this reorganization Aging projects that suffer from technical and organizational legacy, may be better of being "reinvented" through a new project started from scratch than trying to reorganize the old project

There is a need to develop a better understanding of teaming processes and module-team management as well as ways to articulate project management in such contexts.

Proposition 3.9 *Team composition and skills required may vary according to the technical characteristics and difficulties of the project, but also according to the psychological profile of the team leader.*

Proposition 3.10 *If modularity and delegation of responsibility are key at project level, the organization of this delegation and the level of centralization will vary according to the technical dependencies of the modules, but also according to the psychological and professional profile of the project leader.*

This paradoxical situation in which commercial business relies on the existence and durability of non-market activities questions industrial economics. This is clearly related to "competition" questions [7]. As in any cooperative agreement devoted to technology or knowledge development, agents put assets together in a "pre-competitive" phase and share the products of their efforts before coming back to competition [5, 12]. On the contrary, a FLOSS project is an open game in which the list of players is not bounded ex-ante by a cooperative agreement and whose product is a public good that cannot be privately appropriated by the players. This corresponds closely to the formation of a consortium for the production of a standard.[3]

But there is still a need for a better understanding of the link between open-source firms' business models and their investment in the production of open source, when they are at the origin of the project, as said in the previous section, but also when they start contributing to an already existing project. For example, Dahlander and Wallin [14] showed that firms strategically sponsor individuals who occupy a central position in a community, in order to better access distributed skills and aiming to control the direction of development of the related projects. But not all companies invest so much, and this does not explain why and when companies develop an open-source-based business model. Based on the concept of "dynamic capabilities" developed by Teece et al. [51], Jullien and Zimmermann [27, 28] proposed that when a software project is evolving rapidly in terms of features and development, and when there are sufficiently skilled users to propose contributions, an open-source strategy may be valid. The key idea is that a company may be able to propose services based on the *management* of this evolution (support on an official version, ad hoc developments, and assistance to users, or, a so-called "3A" strategy: Insurance (which spells "Assurance" in French), Assistance, Adaptation to users' needs). In that case, a company must control the dynamic asset which is the development community—and this requires a deep involvement in the development of the product as well as in the community. When a product is of less importance to a software company, it may be considered as a complementary asset, and thus, the goal of the company may be to create a consortium to co-develop this component.

Proposition 3.11 *The more central the role of an open-source project in a company's business (i.e., a core asset), the more a company will contribute.*

Proposition 3.12 *Projects that are "stable" (i.e., little development efforts beyond basic maintenance) tend not to attract corporate investment.*

But how should firms organize themselves to capture the feedback from communities? Ågerfalk and Fitzgerald [1] observed that to preserve the coexistence and cooperation of two types of organizations that are based on distant albeit not contradictory rationales, firms must, in a nutshell:

- Not seek to dominate and control process.
- Provide professional management and business expertise.
- Help establish an open and trusted ecosystem.

---

[3]What we mean is that a player offers a standard by developing a software, the other players can adopt and contribute to the development. This "unilateral" adoption is usually called "bandwagon" in the literature on standards (see, for instance Farrell et Saloner, 1985). See Bessen (2002) and Baldwin and Clark [2] for a theoretical analysis of the impact of OSS code architecture on the efficiency of libre development. The latter argues that FLOSS may be seen as a new development "institution" (p. 35 and later).

They view such interaction as osmotic rather than parasitic [13], as the firm's resources reinforce communities' sustainability. But, being able to benefit from the cooperation with an open-source project requires internal reorganization, to allow the internal developers to devote a part of their time to these projects, but also to promote cooperative development culture.

As discussed above, companies exert control on open-source communities by getting involved in open-source communities [20]. Companies do this through sponsorship of selected community members, but they can also do this by having their own developers contribute to open-source projects [46]. A key question is how companies can measure the return on investment of such activity, and how can companies manage the involvement of their in-house developers in open-source communities? Is such involvement guided by a strategic purpose only (as the employees represent the investment of the firm into project), or are other considerations at play, such as the training of employees, the negotiation of some compensations (perks) to attract high profile developers? On the other hand, are open-source participants using their involvement to signal their high profile to potential employers?

Other questions still are related to legal consequences of "collective production." In this context, the rise of open-source foundations is a key development. Such foundations are legal entities that represent an open-source project. They can also be used as an institutional tool to manage the strategic evolution of a project; one example of this is the OpenStack project.

The projects that succeed in Phase 2 can last for years, and even decades (Linux was first released in 1991 and is still actively developed). From one single project, they expand to other projects and markets, and may even create a whole ecosystem of intertwined projects—the so-called LAMP stack is an example of this (Linux, Apache, MySQL, and Perl/Python/PHP, and today also Ruby). The governance of these projects can become increasingly complex, and some new layers appear to deal with it, and with the multiplicity of projects, such as the foundation system, which can handle the legal representation of the projects, as well as their long term governance.

Proposition 3.13 *Projects that become part of a common technology stack will sustain their activity and level of maturity as long as the technology stack as a whole can sustain its activity and level of maturity.*

3.5 Phase 3: Maturity and Beyond

When discussing the maturity phase of open-source projects, it is useful to be able to decide whether a project is in fact in its maturity phase. A number of indicators may point to this, for example, a declining or stable number of contributors, contributions, or new features that are added to the project.

Proposition 3.14 *Projects that are stable in terms of the number of features added/removed will lose developers over time as there is a decreasing amount of work left on the project.*

Evidence suggests that as they age, projects find it harder to recruit and retain newcomers [54], and their organization is said to become increasingly bureaucratic [8]. In that respect, these online open projects appear to follow a trend common to traditional organizations, i.e., a natural tendency toward structural inertia when they get bigger, leading to a growing difficulty to adapt [22].

Proposition 3.15 *Mature FLOSS projects tend to become more bureaucratic and rigid in terms of processes and procedures.*

At the same time, as discussed briefly above, the maturity of a project and its ecosystem may suggest that less feature development is needed, which leads to a reduction of the number of involved contributors. While companies may be attracted to new and emerging projects, as they perceive business opportunities the reverse is true as well. Once companies perceive a decline in business value, companies may drop support altogether, for example, stopping sponsorship or the support of developers to work on the project.

Proposition 3.16 *Companies that no longer perceive a project to be of business value will stop investing in that project.*

But even among these mature projects, some projects, with the Linux kernel being a prime example (over 25 years old) remain attractive to new developers while others, such as Apache, see decreased participation, but without full demise as some level of maintenance activity is still needed. It remains an open question as to whether this variety is simply due to external dynamics (e.g., technology changes including hardware developments that require projects to constantly adapt itself, as is the case for the Linux kernel).

Proposition 3.17 *The continuance of external perturbations leads to continued project activity, even when there is no improvement in terms of functionalities.*

Perhaps, are certain governance structures more appropriate or amenable than others? Perhaps certain ecosystems are more resilient; if so, how, and why? Can projects cease due to increased bureaucracy, and what are some of the consequences for developers and the projects' users? Does formal institutionalization of open-source projects (i.e., the creation of foundations) lead to a higher rate of survival?

In other words, how do organizations deal with what Hirschman [25] called the *exit, voice, and loyalty* phenomenon. When participants in an organization (we consider open-source projects as a type of organization) perceive a decrease in quality or benefit to the member, they can either *exit* (withdraw, quit a job, emigrate, stop participating), or they can *voice* (attempt to repair or improve it, express their complaint, or propose changes). The literature stresses the difficulty with the exit strategy in the case of a company, or a country: it is a type of "point of no return" behavior, implying that beyond the fear of losing a job and the salary that comes with it, the fact that employees (or citizens) do not believe in the possible improvement of the situation. Sentimental attachment to the institution may make this belief and the resulting decision to leave even harder. This situation is different for open-source projects, because contributors may join and leave the community freely and more easily. Community members could temporarily leave a community during a "cooling down" period. For individual (voluntary) contributors there are no direct consequences, such as the loss of a salary, which means there are lower barriers to the exit strategy, and thus individual contributors may be less willing to negotiate a solution. While contributors' reputation might be at stake (depending on whether they left due to a conflict, for example), for companies coming and going as they please would jeopardize their reputation and credibility significantly; rejoining a community after a company pulled out may be very difficult. When companies that play a key role in an open-source community leave, the project's sustainability may be jeopardized.

This analysis could suggest also that:

Proposition 3.18 *A project's core members are the last to abandon a project (they are the most attached to the project), and the peripheral ones the first.*

So, in a nutshell, while in a regular organization (a firm), people may be over loyal (they won't voice when they see a problem, afraid of losing their position), but if they do, they will be very committed to finding a solution; in open-source projects, people will probably voice earlier, but also put less effort in finding a solution (and fork or joint a competitive project instead). At the same time, it is not sure that the core members are the best to see the problems and to fix them (to voice). Companies may will voice, but not too much (and possibly not enough), for they may fear to be seen a willingness to take the control; they may be also more committed to find a solutions, for the project they have invested in to survive

Proposition 3.19 *If a project becomes too bureaucratic while lacking innovation, participants may "voice," but those who resent this most are not those who have decision-making power (i.e., core members), or those with business interests (i.e., companies).*

Proposition 3.20 *If a project accepts that it has to reorganize to regain innovativeness, those who have invested the most (core members and companies) will be the most committed to participate in this reorganization.*

However, it is not clear whether this is what happens in reality. Who voices against the slowdown and proposes solution? If the only developers remaining are those hired by companies, will they be sufficiently motivated to sustain a project? Is it wise for companies to stay involved in such projects from a strategic perspective? What might be some indicators that "predict" such downfall or decline in projects? (Some examples of this could include a decrease in quality or slowdown in bug fixes, etc.) Studies that address contributor behavior, their positions or roles within the project or community, and by drawing careful comparisons with behavior in previous phases may lead to fruitful insights that can help us better understand how to manage these issues.

3.6 Conclusion

Most research on open-source software tends to focus on individual software projects, ignoring the complex interactions between the various types of actors listed above, or what is called in this book an open-source ecosystem. Open-source ecosystems are complex networks of different types of actors at different levels of granularity, including open-source projects that rely on other open-source projects, companies who either start new, or invest in existing open-source projects, open-source communities as collections of developers, and of course individual voluntary developers.

Despite two decades of research on open-source software, there is very little theory that helps to explain how open-source ecosystems "work," evolve, sustain, and decline. There is a considerable body of knowledge on the phenomenon of open source, but much of it is disconnected and has ignored the relationships between different open-source projects and between projects and companies. Studies tend to adopt the sample strategy (either developers or projects) or the field study strategy focusing on specific projects, but there is a distinct lack on open-source ecosystems that study the *interactions* and *dependencies* between projects. Given the increasing level of interest of companies in open-source projects, and also the fact that many companies are built and, indeed, enabled by open-source projects, we believe this is a very significant gap in our knowledge base that urgently requires further research, because this will help to better understand the sustainability of open-source projects and their entire ecosystems.

In this chapter, we have made an initial attempt to develop such a theory of open-source ecosystem "microeconomics," which aims to explain the various forces and behaviors that actors exhibit in open-source ecosystems. This initial theory is by no means complete, nor do we have evidence to support our propositions. However, it does help to structure the phenomenon of open-source ecosystems, drawing on a three-phased model from the so-called S-curve model, and to formulate propositions regarding where and what is to be studied. This three-phased structure to explain the life cycle of open-source projects helps to better understand the chronology of the various challenges that projects face. It also helps to explore the role that companies play in each phase. Furthermore, the structure helps to identify open questions for future research (see Table 3.3).

Finally, the death of a project, and even of an ecosystem, may not be the end of the story [31]. Its technology may survive very long, but it can also generate new ideas, and a part of the developers involved in this former project may use the knowledge they acquired to start something new. For example, the decline of the Geronimo project (a Java/OSGi server runtime environment) seems to have seeded the development of the TomEE project by former Geronimo developers, still within the Apache Foundation projects [55].

Proposition 3.21 *Aging projects that suffer from technical and organizational legacy, may be better of being "reinvented" through a new project started from scratch than trying to reorganize the old project.*

Acknowledgments This work was supported, in part, by Science Foundation Ireland grant 15/SIRG/3293 and 13/RC/2094 and co-funded under the European Regional Development Fund through the Southern and Eastern Regional Operational Programme to Lero—the Irish Software Research Centre (www.lero.ie).

References

1. P.J. Ågerfalk, B. Fitzgerald, outsourcing to an unknown workforce: exploring opensourcing as a global sourcing strategy. MIS Q. **32**, 385–400 (2008)
2. C.Y. Baldwin, K.B. Clark, The architecture of participation: does code architecture mitigate free riding in the open source development model? Manage. Sci. **52**(7) 1116–1127 (2006)
3. A. Barcomb, N. Jullien, P. Meyer, A.L. Olteanu, Integrating managerial preferences into the qualitative multi-criteria evaluation of team members, in *Cases based on Multiple Criteria Decision Making/Aiding methods: Building and Solving Decision Models with Computer Implementations* ed. by S Huber (2018)
4. J. Bessen, Open Source Software: Free Provision of Complex Public Goods. Rapport, Research on Innovation (2005)
5. S. Bhattacharya, S. Guriev, Patents vs. trade secrets: knowledge licensing and spillover. J. Econ. Assoc. **4**(6), 1112–1147 (2006)
6. A. Bonaccorsi, C. Rossi, Why open source software can succeed. Res. Policy **32**(7), 1243–1258 (2003)
7. A. Brandenburger, B. Nalebuff, *Co-Opetition*. (Currency Doubleday, 1996)
8. B. Butler, E. Joyce, J. Pike, Don't look now, but we've created a bureaucracy: the nature and roles of policies and rules in Wikipedia, in *Proceedings of The Twenty-Sixth Annual Sigchi Conference On Human Factors in Computing Systems* (ACM, 2008), pp. 1101–1110
9. K. Carillo, S. Huff, B. Chawner, What makes a good contributor? Understanding contributor behavior within large Free/Open source software projects–a socialization perspective. J. Strateg. Inf. Syst. (2017)
10. E.J. Castilla, S. Benard, The paradox of meritocracy in organizations. Admin. Sci. Q. **55**(4), 543–676 (2010)
11. S. Comino, F.M. Manenti, M.L. Parisi, From planning to mature: on the success of open source projects. Res. Policy **36**, 1575–1586 (2007)
12. J. Crémer, C. d'Aspremont, L.A. Gérard-Varet, Incentives and the existence of pareto-optimal revelation mechanisms. J. Econ. Theory **51**(2), 233–254 (1990)
13. L. Dahlander, M.G. Magnusson, Relationships between open source software companies and communities: observations from nordic firms. Res. Policy **34**, 481–493 (2005)
14. L. Dahlander, M.W. Wallin, A man on the inside: unlocking communities as complementary assets. Res. Policy **35**(8), 1243–1259 (2006)
15. J. Dalle, N. Jullien, 'Libre' software: turning fads into institutions? Res. Policy **32**(1), 1–11 (2003)
16. P. David, A multi-dimensional view of the "sustainability" of free & open source software development, in *OSS Watch Conference on Open Source and Sustainability* (Saïd Business School, Oxford, 2006), pp. 10–12
17. J. Dedrick, J. West, An exploratory study into open source platform adoption, in *Proceedings of the 37th Annual Hawaii International Conference on System Sciences (HICSS)* (2004)
18. N. Eghbal, *Roads and Bridges: The Unseen Labor Behind Our Digital Infrastructure* (2016). Accessed from https://www.fordfoundation.org
19. J. Farrell, Standardization and intellectual property. Jurimetr. J. **30**, 35 (1989)
20. M. Germonprez, J.E. Kendall, K.E. Kendall, L. Mathiassen, B.W. Young, B. Warner, A theory of responsive design: a field study of corporate engagement with open source communities. Inf. Syst. Res. **28**(1), 64–83 (2017)

21. R. Guimera, B. Uzzi, J. Spiro, L.A.N. Amaral, Team assembly mechanisms determine collaboration network structure and team performance. Science **308**(5722), 697–702 (2005)
22. M.T. Hannan, J. Freeman, Structural inertia and organizational change, Am. Soc. Rev. **49**(2), 149–164 (1984)
23. D.D. Heckathorn, The dynamics and dilemmas of collective action. Am. Soc. Rev. **61**(2), 278–307 (1996)
24. C. Hess, E. Ostrom, Introduction: an overview of the knowledge commons, in*Understanding Knowledge as a Commons: From Theory to Practice*, ed. by C. Hess, E. Ostrom (MIT Press, 2007)
25. A.O. Hirschman, *Exit, Voice, and Loyalty: Responses to Decline in Firms, Organizations, and States*, vol. 25 (Harvard University Press, Cambridge, 1970)
26. C. Jensen, W. Scacchi, Role migration and advancement processes in ossd projects: a comparative case study, in *29th International Conference on Software Engineering (ICSE'07)*, Minneapolis, MN, USA, pp. 364–374 (2007)
27. N. Jullien, J.B. Zimmermann, FLOSS firms, users and communities: a viable match? J. Innov. Econ. Manag. **1**, 31–53 (2011)
28. N. Jullien, J.B. Zimmermann, FLOSS in an industrial economics perspective. Revue d'économie industrielle **136**(4), 39–64 (2011)
29. Jullien, K. Roudaut, Can Open Source projects succeed when the producers are not users? Lessons from the data processing field. Manag. Int./Int. Manag./Gestiòn Int. **16**, 113–127 (2012)
30. J.E. Kendall, K.E. Kendall, M. Germonprez, Game theory and open source contribution: rationale behind corporate participation in open source software development. J. Organ. Comput. Electron. Commer. **26** (4), 323–343 (2016)
31. J. Khondhu, A. Capiluppi, K.J. Stol, Is it all lost? A study of inactive open source projects, in *Proceedings of IFIP International Conference on Open Source Systems* (2013), pp. 61–79
32. S. Koch, Organisation of work in open source projects: expended effort and efficiency. Revue d'économie industrielle **136**, 17–38 (2011)
33. B. Kogut, A. Metiu, Open source software development and distributed innovation. Oxf. Rev. Econ. Policy **17**(2), 248–264 (2001)
34. M.C. Lacity, S.A. Khan, L.P. Willcocks, A review of the IT outsourcing literature: Insights for practice. J. Strateg. Inf. Syst. **18**(3), 130–146 (2009)
35. K. Lakhani, R. Wolf, Why hackers do what they do: understanding motivation and effort in free/open source software projects, in *Perspectives on Free and Open Source Software, ed. by* J. Feller, B. Fitzgerald, S. Hissam, K.R. Lakhani (MIT Press, Cambridge, 2005)
36. K. Lakhani, E. von Hippel, How open source software works: free user to user assistance. Res. Policy **32**(6), 923–943 (2003)
37. G. Marwell, P. Oliver, *The Critical Mass in Collective Action* (Cambridge University Press, Cambridge, 1993). Discusses user as producer involvement into a project (a collective action)
38. A. Mockus, R.T. Fielding, J. Herbsleb, A case study of open source software development: the Apache server, in *Proceedings of the 22nd International Conference on Software Engineering* (ACM, 2000, June), pp. 263–272
39. L. Morgan, J. Feller, P. Finnegan, Exploring value networks: theorising the creation and capture of value with open source software. Eur. J. Inf. Syst. **22**, 569–588 (2013)
40. D. Nafus, 'Patches don't have gender': what is not open in open source software. New Media Soc. **14**(4), 669–683 (2012)
41. P.V. Norden, On the anatomy of development projects. IRE Trans. Eng. Manag. **7**(1), 34–42 (1960)
42. P. Oliver, G. Marwell, R. Teixeira, A theory of the critical mass. I. Interdependence, group heterogeneity, and the production of collective action. Am. J. Soc. **91**(3), 522–556 (1985)
43. E.S. Raymond, *The Cathedral and the Bazaar* (O'Reilly Media, Sebastopol, 2001)
44. J. Reagle, "Free as in sexist?" Free culture and the gender gap. First Monday **18**(1) (2012)
45. E.M. Rogers, New Product Adoption and Diffusion. J. Consum. Res. **2**(4), 290–301 (1976)

46. M. Schaarschmidt, K.J. Stol, Company soldiers and gone-natives: role conflict and career ambition among firm-employed open source developers, in *Proceedings of the 39th International Conference on Information Systems* (San Francisco, USA)

47. M. Schaarschmidt, G. Walsh, H.F.O. von Kortzfleisch, How do firms influence open source software communities? A framework and empirical analysis of different governance modes. Inf. Organ. **25**, 99–114 (2015)

48. M. Shaikh, T. Cornford, 'Letting go of control' to embrace open source: implications for company and community, in *Proceedings of IEEE Hawaii International Conference on System Sciences (HICSS)* (2010)

49. K.J. Stewart, S. Gosain, The impact of ideology on effectiveness in open source software development teams. MIS Q. **30**(2), 291–314 (2006)

50. G.P. Swann, *The economics of standardization* (University of Manchester, Manchester, 2000)

51. D.J. Teece, G. Pisano, A. Shuen, Dynamic capabilities and strategic management. Strateg. Manag. J. **18**, 509–533 (1997)

52. F. Van der Linden, B. Lundell, P. Marttiin, Commodification of industrial software: a case for open source. IEEE Softw. **26**(4), 77–83 (2009)

53. E. von Hippel, G. von Krogh, Open source software and the "private-collective" innovation model: issues for organization science. Organ. Sci. **14**(2), 209–223 (2003)

54. G. Von Krogh, S. Spaeth, K.R. Lakhani, Community, joining, and specialization in open source software innovation: a case study. Res. Policy **32**(7), 1217–1241 (2003)

55. M. Zhou, A. Mockus, X. Ma, L. Zhang, M. Hong, Inflow and retention in oss communities with commercial involvement: a case study of three hybrid projects. ACM Trans. Softw. Eng. Methodol. **25**(2), 13 (2016)

Chapter 4
Open-Source Ecosystems and Their Need for a Legal Framework

Daniel M. German

Abstract Open source cannot exist without open-source licenses. The main purpose of an open-source license is to grant a set of rights to the users of the software (such as running the software or creating derivative works from it). There exist many open-source licenses today, each with its own set of rights and conditions. Each of these licenses creates a social contract between the licensors of the software (usually its creators) and its users, and become the legal foundation upon which the ecosystem around the software system is created. This article describes how open source, their ecosystems, and their licenses are intimately related, and how the evolution of one affects the evolution of the others. Over time, open-source licenses are being created to adapt to the needs of open-source ecosystems and to adapt to changes in the legal environment too.

4.1 Introduction

The simplest—and most effective—definition of open-source software is software that is licensed under an open-source license. This definition shifts the definition from the technical domain to the legal one, but more importantly, emphasizes that without open-source licenses there would be no open-source software. The Open Source Initiative (OSI) defined the characteristics that an open-source license should have [9], and has approved 82 licenses as open source [8]. Nonetheless, many other licenses exist that arguably satisfy the requirements defined by OSI (such as the License of Ruby, and the *Do What the Fuck You Want To Public License*) [4, 22].

The ecosystem of open source is very large and it is not a single monolithic entity. This ecosystem is composed, among others, of the many (smaller) ecosystems that are created around each of the different open-source software systems. In these smaller ecosystems, their members participate with the expectation of gaining one or more benefits in return. These benefits might be, among others, ethical (the good feeling of

D. M. German (✉)
University of Victoria, Victoria, Canada
e-mail: dmg@turingmachine.org

© Springer Nature Singapore Pte Ltd. 2019
B. Fitzgerald et al. (eds.), *Towards Engineering Free/Libre Open Source Software (FLOSS) Ecosystems for Impact and Sustainability*,
https://doi.org/10.1007/978-981-13-7099-1_4

helping others), educational (experience gained in the use of certain technologies), or pecuniary (direct or indirect revenue derived from participating in the ecosystem).

The license of an open-source system lays the foundation on top of which ecosystems of open-source systems are created. It explains how the users can benefit (or not) from development, use, and exploitation of the software system. For some, participating in a particular ecosystem might also be an ideological act, which in some cases might be emphasized by the text of the license (for example, the preamble of the General Public License–GPL—addresses political issues beyond intellectual property law). For others, it does not matter how the software is used (the Do What the Fuck You Want To Public License—WTFPL—states that the copyright owners of the system have no interest on what others do with the software, but want to keep its copyright—rather than place the software in the public domain). Netscape, when it open sourced its Navigator, found that no license satisfied its need, as a corporation, for potential commercial exploitation and created its own license, the Netscape Public License. This license, and its derivatives—the different versions of the Mozilla Public License—explicitly define what commercial use is.

The following sections make the argument that licenses and open-source ecosystems are symbiotic: one cannot exist without the other. The ecosystem is created around a license; however, as the ecosystem evolves, it creates the need to adapt its license to its new needs of the ecosystem. However, licenses are often not enough, and ecosystems need to complement them with a proper organization (a foundation), whose purpose is to create a framework in which the different entities of the ecosystem can collaborate together to further the success of the software system.

4.2 Building an Ecosystem of Users and Developers: The Need for a License

Open software ecosystems can be traced back to the early days of computing. According to the Wikipedia [29], early users of computers shared software and collaborated in its improvement as if it was in the public domain. Computers were shipped with the source code of their operating systems, allowing users to debug it, customize it, and improve it.

One important moment in the history of open-source licensing was the early days of Emacs, the customizable editor, one of the oldest open-source software applications still in use today. Emacs was created by Richard Stallman in 1975 [16, 17]. As of 1981, the (very informal) license of Emacs read:

> [Emacs] is distributed on a basis of communal sharing, which means that all improvements must be given back to be incorporated and distributed.

The success of Emacs prompted many to port it to other platforms and to create new implementations from scratch. One of these ports was the first implementations of Emacs for Unix, written by James Gosling (creator of Java) [18]. Originally, Gosling allowed others to redistribute and modify his implementation. By then an ecosystem of users and developers existed, whose goal was to keep improving Emacs. Stallman argues that a major part of the success of Emacs was the feedback loop between users and developers and that Emacs was the first extensible editor, allowing users to become developers of extensions to the editor [16]. Gosling was an eager member of this Emacs community; according to Stallman [16]: "[Gosling] wrote in a manual that he called the program Emacs hoping that others in the community would improve it until it was worthy of that name."

Stallman reused some of Gosling's code in his own port of Emacs for Unix, GNU Emacs (the first project released by the GNU Project) [27]. However, in 1983 Gosling sold the rights to his code to Unipress. Immediately after, Unipress asked Stallman to stop using any code from Gosling's Emacs (Stallman complied). A major outcome of these events was Stallman's realization that, in order to guarantee the spirit of communal work that he envisioned, he had to draft a proper copyright license for Emacs. This license became the GNU Emacs Public License and it evolved to become the GNU General Public License, published in 1988.

4.3 A Software System, Its Licensing, and Its Ecosystem

It can be argued that any software system creates an ecosystem around it. At its minimum, the ecosystem is composed of the developer (or developers) and its users. Larger ecosystems are composed of many different types of actors. For example, it might include intermediaries (such as the store where the users acquire the software), entities providing training and support, developers who might create plug-ins to improve the features of the software, and many different types of users. In this context, an ecosystem might also include a place for exchange of knowledge or ideas (e.g., a tag in StackOverflow or Quora, or a mailing list), and a market (where services and products are exchanged for some type of consideration).

A user requires a license to be able to use the software system. There might also be a fee associated in the acquisition of such license. This license imposes some rights and obligations, usually related to copyright law. At the minimum it will allow the user to run the program, often with specific constraints. It might restrict its use for certain purposes,[1] limit the number of users that can run it, or the number of times it can be run, or limit the period of time when the software can be run. In some cases, the license might even impose limitations on the output of the software, even if the output involves the user. For example, it is not uncommon for licenses to forbid the use of the software to create a competing product (such as BitKeeper, the version control system used by Linux in the early 2000s did; similarly, the license of Bison, a compiler of compilers developed by the Free Software Foundation, imposes some limitations on its use for the creation of compilers of compilers).

However, a license—particularly an open-source license–can also widely expand the rights of how the software can be used that otherwise are forbidden by copyright

---

[1] For example, some licenses do not allow the software to be run for benchmarking purposes.

law. For example, the right to run the software for any purpose, the right to create copies of the software and distribute them for free or for a fee, the right to resell or give away the software, the right to create derivative works, etc.

In essence, the license determines a basic set of rules under which the actors in the ecosystem can participate. For example, an entity interested in providing training for the software must be able to acquire a license that allows it to run the software for such purpose. A developer interested in improving the software requires a license that allows such improvements, either as plug-ins (this would also require an architecture that supports this feature) or by modifying the underlying software.

Contracts are often the legal mechanism used to grant a license to a user (their most common type is known as End-User Agreement). Another legal mechanism is pure copyright licenses, that do not require a legal agreement between the two parties (such as the license one acquires when one buys an album or a movie). Other contracts that apply to the software might not be related to how users use the software, but how other actors can participate in the ecosystem. For example, a retailer might have a contract that guarantees it to be the exclusive entity that can market and sell the software system.

4.4   GPL and Free Software: Software by the Users to the Users

The ecosystem that Richard Stallman envisioned in his GNU Manifesto [13] is summarized in the Four Freedoms of Free Software, which are the cornerstone of his movement: the freedom to run the program as you wish, the freedom to study how the program works (access to the source code), the freedom to redistribute copies, and the freedom to modify the program and redistribute copies of modified program. "Roughly it means the users have the freedom to run, copy, distribute, study, change and improve the software." [21]. Free Software is software that guarantees its users these four freedoms.

Stallman had described how for-profit entities had started to make it difficult to improve and share software [14]. In his view, software is by the users for the users. In [23], he writes: "we designed the GNU General Public License (GNU GPL) to release [the GNU Project software systems] under a license designed specifically to protect freedom for all users of a program." Hence, the GPL lays the legal foundation in which an ecosystem can guarantee that software will be Free Software, and that users will retain their four freedoms. Users (and developers) flocked to this ecosystem and its success is without question.

When Linus Torvalds released his first version of Linux, he was concerned with issues similar to those that had affected Stallman: he was worried that for-profit entities would unfairly benefit from his software without remunerating his work. The first release of Linux (version 0.01, 1991) comes with an ad hoc license created by Linus requiring that any redistribution (in full or in part) should make all the source code available, copyright notices should be left intact, and no fee can be charged for redistribution [32]. Linus starts the creation of a kernel as an effort of a user, to the users, in a similar manner than Stallman had started the GNU Project before him (Linus benefited tremendously from the GNU Project: he included many of the GNU tools along with his kernel, so users could use his kernel). Linus soon realized the benefits of joining the ecosystem created by the FSF, and in 1992 changed the license of Linux to the GPL-2: "Making Linux GPL'd was definitely the best thing I ever did" [35].

At first sight, Free Software might be intended to alienate for-profit entities. Cygnus Solutions was one of the first participants of this type to join this ecosystem (it merged with RedHat in 2000). According to its founder, Michael Tiemann, the FSF ecosystem created a business opportunity [31]: "companies that provided commercial services (customizations, enhancements, bug fixes, support) based on that [Free] [S]oftware could capitalize on the economies of scale and broad appeal of this new kind of software." Cygnus Solutions took advantage of this opportunity and became, by 1998, the largest open-source company in the world [31].

For-profit entities were welcome to join the ecosystem, as long as their participation keeps the Free Software guarantee to its users (i.e., it follows its license). While they are able to sell copies of software they create, others can then copy them many times again without having to pay an extra fee. In other words, they can only expect to profit from the first sell, but the ecosystem welcomes their participation in selling services around free software. Today, most Free Software reaches users through for-profit entities who sell it as part of hardware devices (TVs, routers, embedded devices, all using Android or, Linux) or as distributions of GNU/Linux (RedHat, Ubuntu, Suse). Even Apple's OS X distributes a large collection of Free Software.

4.5   The Academic Licenses: Do as you Wish

An early realization of Stallman is that his employment precluded his ability to create Free Software. In most jurisdictions, in the absence of any other agreement, the employer is the owner of the intellectual property created by the employee. This was one of the reasons that he quit MIT in 1984 [13].

Others were faced with similar challenges: how to create software that could be shared and enhanced by others, without the constraints that intellectual property law imposed? The solution came in the form of academic licenses, that allow the copyright holder (usually an academic institution) to relinquish most intellectual property rights to the software.

One of the oldest of these licenses is the MIT/X11. In the 1980s, MIT researchers were working on the creation of a GUI interface for Unix computers called X-Window System (X, for short). The project, called Athena, was jointly sponsored by DEC, IBM, and MIT. Both IBM and DEC built Unix computers at the time and were fighting with each other for a share of the Unix marketplace; however, they realized that working together to create a GUI for Unix they could increase the size of the market—which, in the long term, would benefit both companies. Athena created an ecosystem in which academics and for-profit participants worked together with a common goal. It is likely that MIT researchers, DEC and IBM wanted to benefit from any software being developed, but at the same time foster an ecosystem in which others (individuals and organizations) would feel welcome to collaborate in its further development. The solution was to draft a license that allowed anybody to do anything they wished with the software—that was otherwise forbidden by copyright law—as long as the copyright notices in the files were not removed. This license became known as MIT/X11, and today is one of the most popular open-source licenses.

Researchers at University of California, Berkeley had a similar challenge while developing a new version of Unix called the Berkeley Software Distribution (BSD). The academic operating systems community (specially the Unix community) was being encumbered by intellectual property issues that limited their ability to share and enhance the works of others. In 1988, Version 4.3BSD-Tahoe of BSD is released under a license that is likely derived from the MIT/X11. Its main difference is the restriction that the name of the University (the copyright holder) "may not be used to endorse or promote products derived from this software without specific prior written permission" [26]. This license would eventually become the BSD-4, and further derived into the BSD-3 and BSD-2 licenses.

These licenses, the MIT/X11 and the BSD-4, create ecosystems where the software is for anybody to use, for whatever purpose. They welcome for-profit organizations who do not need to feel restricted in the way they participate in the system. These organizations could take the software, further modified it and sell it, without any requirement to share the improvements or profits.

The MIT/X11 and BSD-4 licenses influenced the University of Illinois/NCSA Open Source License (UIUC) that was used in the HTTP server that NCSA (located at the University of Illinois) was developing. This license was likely one of the major reasons that this server became popular and—arguably—partially responsible for the success of the World Wide Web. Such was the success in the creation of an ecosystem around httpd, that its development was taken over by its users, creating in 1995 the Apache HTTP Server,[2] the most successful Web server to date [5]. The creation of Apache HTTP Server was possible because the license of NCSA's http server allowed it.

4.6   The Other IPs: Trademarks and Patents

As the success of Apache HTTP Server continued, it developers noted the need to protect its name. This is likely among the reasons they changed its license and release the Server under the Apache License version 1.0 (and later, version 1.1). The main difference between the adapted BSD license (from which it is derived) is the addition

---

[2]It is often mentioned that its name is short for "A PATCHy sErver" in reference to its origins as a set of patches on top of the NCSA server.

of the following clause that protects the name of the software system (present in both versions of the license):

> Products derived from this software may not be called "Apache" nor may "Apache" appear in their names without prior written permission of the Apache Group.

It appears that one of the advantages of the permissiveness of the original Apache License was also its disadvantage: it allowed members of the ecosystem to commercialize the software system, even under the Apache name, creating confusion among other participants of the ecosystem. Avoiding this type of confusion is one of the major goals of trademarks.[3]

IBM, as a leader in the field, was also starting to experiment with this nascent method to develop and distribute software. However, IBM did not embrace any of the licenses at the time and decided to create its own, the IBM Public License (IPL). The main differences of this license with respect to its predecessors are: placing liability not on the creator of the software but on the distributor, and the addition of clauses that specifically address patents. The software that used this license had little impact, but the IPL became the predecessor of the Common Public License (CPL) that later evolved into the Eclipse Public License (EPL).

4.7 Open Source: The Need to Create a Larger Ecosystem

The proliferation of licenses for these open projects was creating barriers for collaboration between their corresponding ecosystems, even though they had similar goals in mind: to collaborate in the development of software where the source code could be openly shared, enhanced, and redistributed (with or without enhancements). Furthermore, many of these licenses were considered incompatible with each other (e.g., the original BSD-4 license and all GPL versions are incompatible) restricting the potential sharing of software between the different ecosystems [2]. Nonetheless, new ecosystems were being created around these software projects (and their ecosystems), such as Linux distributions—most notably Debian. Debian's goal has been to create a Free Software operating system. One of the major challenges that Debian faced was the evaluation of different licenses to determine if they were Free Software (this process is documented in the Debian Free Software Guidelines [20]). Debian is one of the first to try to harmonize different software products under the umbrella of Free Software. By doing this, it enlarges the ecosystem by integrating Free Software developed under difference licenses,

In 1999, the Open Source Initiative (OSI) is created with two major goals in mind [7]. The first is to define a new term, Open Source, that formalizes many of the goals of the communities around these open collaboration systems; this goal is accomplished with the Open Source Definition, a set of 10 requirements that a software license must have to be called Open Source (these requirements are derived

---

[3]This need to protect the name of Apache was one of the major motivators for the creation of the Apache Software Foundation [1].

from the Debian Free Software Guidelines). The second is the creation of a certi-fication process by which licenses can be approved to be called *Open Source*. The term Open Source was also created to "distinguish it from the philosophically—and politically-focused label 'Free Software.' [7] and to incorporate under its umbrella licenses that were not considered to be Free Software, but that satisfied the basic requirements of open collaboration (such as the BSD-4 or the EPL). The term Open Source unifies all the communities behind each of the projects that use any of the OSI-approved licenses under a larger ecosystem: the Open-Source community.

The success of Open Source prompted the interest of for-profit organizations to participate in the Open-Source ecosystems—and to benefit from them. License compliance has become a necessity for these organizations; they want to make sure that, if they use Open Source, they do it in the correct way—first and foremost—by satisfying the requirements that the licenses of the software they use. License com-pliance has become an important concern for those using Open Source (specially when the goal is to make profit). This has lead to the creation of for-profit organi-zations that assist others in license compliance (Black Duck is today the leader in this area) and community efforts to create resources to educate developer and orga-nizations on best practices. For example, the Linux Foundation has been sponsoring efforts toward license compliance, such as the Software Package Data Exchange format—SPDX, whose goal is to standardize how licensing information should be shared between organizations using Open-Source software [12] and the Open Com-pliance Program [25], whose goal is to educate and help developers and companies to properly comply with license requirements.

Other organizations were created by the authors of Open-Source software with the explicit goal of guaranteeing that those using the software comply with its license. The most important being GPL Violations, whose goal is to raise awareness regarding infringement of GPLed software, and to assist developers in the enforcement of their copyrights [34].

4.8   The Foundations: The Need to Go Beyond the License

In 1985, the Free Software Foundation is formed to create a legal structure around its software [28]. It holds the copyright of a major portion of the software developed by the FSF, accepts donations to continue its development, and is the steward of the GPL family of licenses.

Apache HTTP Server became so successful at creating an ecosystem around it, that it required a formalized way to organize its users. In 1999, the Apache Foundation is established. Four of its most important reasons for existence are [1]: to provide hardware and business support to the community of developers, to serve as a legal entity that can receive donations, to shield members from potential legal risks, and to protect the Apache trademark.

Over the years, many other foundations have been created. Some by individuals for the individuals (e.g., GNOME Foundation, the Software Freedom Conservancy), others by for-profit companies interested in creating an independent entity to anchor the growing ecosystem (e.g., KDE e.V., the Eclipse Foundation), and finally, as a consortium of for-profit organizations to collaboratively foster the ecosystem's development (e.g., The Linux Foundation, the OpenStack Foundation).

While the bylaws of each of these organizations differ, they all have one feature in common: they become the center of activity around the software system (or systems), and by extension, the center of their corresponding ecosystems.

Some foundations also create a strong set of rules that determine how other software systems join the ecosystem. For example, both, the Apache Foundation and the Open Stack Foundation have strong rules in terms of how a new software system can become part of its ecosystem. This includes what license is should have (e.g., Apache Foundation only accepts software systems that use the Apache License or a license compatible with it [19]).

4.9 License Evolution: The Need to Adapt to the Environment

As time passes by, the license used by a software system becomes inadequate to address the needs of its ecosystem, specially those of its main contributors and users. For example, the GNU GCC compiler, one of the first Free Software projects, generates binaries that need an implementation of the C standard library to run. Without this library, C programs are not very useful. The GCC project faced two alternatives: write its own C Standard library, or generate code that could have been linked to somebody else's C Standard library. The second alternative as impractical: it would have eroded the freedoms of its users, since it would have made GNU GCC dependent on acquiring a license to such C Standard library (there was no Free Software implementation at the time). The first alternative meant that this library would have been licensed under the GPL too. If the license of the library was the GPL, then any binary compiled against it would have to be licensed under the GPL too. Effectively, GNU GCC would only be usable to build Free Software. This issue raised interesting ethical concerns: *should Free software be only used to create Free Software only?* or, *should the person who runs the software have the* freedom *to create binaries under a different license?* It became obvious that for GNU GCC to succeed (and it did succeed) users should be allowed to do anything they wanted with the binaries they created. The ecosystem for GNU GCC needed to grow beyond the restrictions imposed by the GPL. According to Richard Stallman, "using the GPL for [the GCC C Standard library] would have driven proprietary software developers to use another [compiler]" [15].

The solution was the creation of the Library General Public License (today known as the Lesser General Public License–LGPL). The LGPL is primarily designed to be used by a library, and it allows a program that links to such library to have any license. The LPGL tries to achieve a balance between the goals of Free Software (the library cannot be modified without making these modifications Free Software) and the needs of proprietary software (to create software that they can license—and sell—as its owner pleases.

There are many other instances in which licenses have evolved due to the needs of its users. One of the major motivations for the creation of the GPL-3 was the need to address patents. The Apache License 1.1 removes the main advertising clause, present in version 1.0, something that made it difficult to commercialize products based upon it. The IBM Public License evolved into the Common Public License because of the need to remove IBM from the license text, hence making the license usable by others.

As mentioned before, licenses, when incompatible between each other, foster isolation of their ecosystems. The original BSD-4 license is incompatible with the GPL family of licenses. Software developed under this license cannot be combined into derivative works under the GPL license. The Mozilla Public License version 1 and the Eclipse Public License are also incompatible with the GPL. Even worse is that some licenses are incompatible with licenses in their same family. Software licensed under the GPL-2 is incompatible with software licensed under the GPL-3.[4]

However, if the goal of Open Source is to create software that can be shared, enhanced, and further distributed, license incompatibilities have become a barrier between communities, sometimes in ironic ways: any organization can enhance and further distribute code under the BSD-4 and license the results under a restrictive license, yet a software project licensed under the GPL cannot do it. License compatibility has been one of the major reasons licenses have been updated. For example, the Mozilla Public License 2.0 added clauses that explicitly address compatibility with the GPL family of licenses.

4.10   Fairness: Rules on How to Collaborate

Any ecosystem is expected to have internal struggles between its participants, and open-source ecosystems are not an exception. This struggle is, perhaps, one of the major contributors to its natural evolution and adaption—without it, it might simply cease to exist.

The FSF has been, since its conception, concerned with keeping the entire copyright of its most important software systems. This guarantees the FSF the ability to relicense the software in any way its sees fit (usually, by changing the license to a new version of the GPL). Contributors to FSF's software are requested to transfer their copyright of their improvements; otherwise these improvements will not be incorporated. This position has lead to split of ecosystems. When some Emacs developers

---

[4]This is the reason why the Free Software Foundation recommends that software be licensed under *the General Public License version 3 or any further version*; this way, when a new version of the license is published, software can be relicensed under the new version, making it unnecessary for the new version to be compatible with the older one.

were not willing (or capable, since their copyrights were sometimes owned by their employers) they created XEmacs, dividing the Emacs community and its ecosystem [30]. See [6] for a study of the motivations of developers to fork, which includes licensing issues.

In other ecosystems, the struggles have been around control. For example, the Gnome Project was very concerned that for-profit organizations could hijack the project from its users. The main body responsible for making decisions is the Board of Directors of the Gnome Foundation. The bylaws of the Gnome Foundation state that no "organization, corporation or similar entity, or any affiliate of shall hold more than 40% of the Board [of Directors] seats" [24]. Other ecosystems, primarily those created by for-profit organizations, see it differently and give more power to specific entities. For example, the Open Stack Foundation categorizes members into three types: individuals, Platinum (further divided into Class A and B), and Gold. Platinum members, which have to pay higher fees than Gold members, receive certain privileges in return (each Platinum member can appoint a member for the Board of Directors, while Gold members are represented by persons who are voted whom they vote for [10]).

The difference between the structure and organization of the Board of Directors of these foundations highlights the typical struggles of distributive fairness found in any collaborative environment. Distributive fairness is concerned with how resources should be allocated to each member of a system (see [3] for a description of fairness within the scope of software engineering). On one hand, a system can strive for equality: each member should have the same benefits as any other member, regardless of its amount of participation (as Gnome does, where any contributor can be a member of the foundation and be elected to its Board of Directors–the Gnome Foundation bylaws define the process and minimum requirements to achieve membership). On the other hand, a system can strive for equity: each member receives a benefit from the system that is proportional to its participation (as Open Stack does, where does who contribute more—Platinum members, who pay a membership of 500k US$, compared to Gold members who pay at most 200k US$ [11]—receive more benefits from the system, in this case their ability to control the project's direction). It is not clear if one system is better than the other, but it certainly affects the decision-making process of their corresponding ecosystems.

Another important type of fairness is interactional fairness. Interactional fairness is concerned with the interpersonal treatment of people in a system. It reflects the degree to which people are treated with politeness, dignity, and respect. While merit has been seen as the main factor that determined membership and status in an Open-Source ecosystem, it became clear that it was necessary to create rules that defined how people were to treat others. As described by Tourani et al., each ecosystem addresses this issue in a different way: "the phrasing of a code of conduct, enforcement mechanisms used, scope and other properties vary depending on the code of conduct and [its] community" [33].

The rise of the foundations around open-source systems, the decision processes and the code of conduct rules that these projects select demonstrates that the licenses—a prerequisite of an Open-Source ecosystem—are not necessarily sufficient to guarantee the successful collaboration of its members.

4.11   Conclusion

The license of an Open-Source system becomes the legal framework that outlines the rights and responsibilities of the ecosystem participants. Without an Open-Source license, and Open-Source system cannot exist, nor its ecosystem. With the pass of time, the needs of the main stakeholders of the ecosystem evolve, which might force a change in its license.

The creation of a foundation is a major landmark in the evolution of an ecosystem. It legally formalizes the relationship between the different members of the ecosystem, and its decision process. The bylaws of a foundation (a legal document itself) complement the license of its system. A foundation is capable of changing the license of the system (and often changes it) in response to the needs of its members.

Projects have also complemented the rules of participation with rules of conduct. These rules might not be legally enforceable, but give the ecosystem the ability to expel a noncompliant member.

The nature of any social ecosystem requires rules that outline its members participate, collaborate, and benefit from it. Ecosystems have flourished around open-source systems because their licenses have created the social contract that guarantees that the needs of its members are satisfied. And when licenses have stopped doing this, the ecosystems find ways to adjust, because, after all, an ecosystem's goal is to continue flourishing.

References

1. Apache Software Foundation, Frequently asked questions (2017), http://apache.org/foundation/faq.html
2. D.M. German, A.E. Hassan, License integration patterns: addressing license mismatches in component-based development, in *31st International Conference on Software Engineering, ICSE 2009* (16–24 May 2009 Vancouver, Canada, Proceedings), pp. 188–198
3. D.M. German, G. Robles, G. Poo-Caamaño, X. Yang, H. Iida, K. Inoue, "Was my contribution fairly reviewed?": a framework to study the perception of fairness in modern code reviews, in *Proceedings of the 40th International Conference on Software Engineering, ICSE 2018* (Gothenburg, Sweden, 27 May–03 June, 2018), pp. 523–534
4. R.M. Meloca, G. Pinto, L. Baiser, M. Mattos, I. Polato, I.S. Wiese, D.M. German, Understanding the usage, impact, and adoption of non-osi approved licenses, in *Proceedings of the 15th International Conference on Mining Software Repositories, MSR 2018* (Gothenburg, Sweden, 28–29 May 2018)

5. Netcraft Inc. July 2017 Web Server Survey (2017), https://news.netcraft.com/archives/2017/07/20/july-2017-web-server-survey.html, July 2017
6. L. Nyman, T. Mikkonen, To fork or not to fork: fork motivations in sourceforge projects, in *Open Source Systems: Grounding Research: 7th IFIP WG 2.13 International Conference, OSS 2011, Salvador, Brazil, 6–7 Oct 2011. Proceedings*, ed. by S.A. Hissam, B. Russo, M.G. de Mendonça Neto, F. Kon (Springer, Berlin, Heidelberg, 2011), pp. 259–268
7. Open Source Initiative, History of the OSI (1998), https://opensource.org/history
8. Open Source Initiative, Licenses by name (1998), https://opensource.org/licenses/alphabetical
9. Open Source Initiative, The Open Source Definition (1998), https://opensource.org/osd
10. Open Stack Foundation, Bylaws of the OpenStack Foundation (2014), https://www.openstack.org/legal/bylaws-of-the-openstack-foundation/
11. Open Stack Foundation, Proposed Budget and Funding Structure (2017), https://wiki.openstack.org/wiki/Governance/Foundation/Funding
12. SPDX Working Group, About The Software Package Data Exchange SPDX (2017), https://spdx.org/
13. R. Stallman, The GNU Manifesto. Dr. Dobb's Journal of Software Tools (1985), http://www.drdobbs.com/open-source/the-gnu-manifesto/222200498, Sep 1985
14. R. Stallman, The GNU Operating System and the Free Software Movement, *Open Sources: Voices from the Open Source Revolution*, 1st edn. (O'Reilly, Sebastopol, Jan 1999)
15. R. Stallman, Why you shouldn't use the Lesser GPL for your next library (2017), https://www.gnu.org/licenses/why-not-lgpl.en.html
16. R.M. Stallman, *Emacs: The extensible, customizable, self-documenting display editor*, Technical report (Massachusetts Institute of Technology, Cambridge, 1979)
17. R.M. Stallman, Emacs the extensible, customizable self-documenting display editor, in *Proceedings of the ACM SIGPLAN SIGOA Symposium on Text Manipulation* (ACM, New York, USA, 1981), pp. 147–156
18. L.-C.A. Ta, The History of the GPL (2001), https://www.free-soft.org/gpl_history/, July 2001
19. The Apache Software Foundation, Incubation Policy (2017), http://incubator.apache.org/incubation/Incubation_Policy.html
20. The Debian Project. Debian Social Contract version 1.0 (1997), https://www.debian.org/social_contract.1.0, July 1997
21. The Free Software Foundation, What is free software? (2016), https://www.gnu.org/philosophy/free-sw.en.html
22. The Free Software Foundation, Various Licenses and Comments about Them (2017), https://www.gnu.org/licenses/license-list.en.html
23. The Free Software Foundation, Why Open Source misses the point of Free Software (2017), https://www.gnu.org/philosophy/open-source-misses-the-point.en.html
24. The GNOME Foundation, Bylaws of GNOME Foundation as of April 5, 2002, https://www.gnome.org/wp-content/uploads/2012/02/bylaws.pdf, Apr 2002
25. The Linux Foundation, About the Open Compliance Program (2017), https://compliance.linuxfoundation.org/about-open-compliance-program
26. The Wikipedia Foundation, Berkeley software distribution (2017), https://en.wikipedia.org/wiki/Berkeley_Software_Distribution
27. The Wikipedia Foundation, Emacs (2017), https://en.wikipedia.org/wiki/Emacs
28. The Wikipedia Foundation. Free Software Foundation (2017), https://en.wikipedia.org/wiki/Free_Software_Foundation
29. The Wikipedia Foundation, History of free and open-source software (2017), https://en.wikipedia.org/wiki/History_of_free_and_open-source_software
30. The Wikipedia Foundation, Xemcas (2017), https://en.wikipedia.org/wiki/XEmacs
31. M. Tiemann, Future of Cygnus Solutions—An Entrepreneur's Account, *Open Sources: Voices from the Open Source Revolution*, 1st edn. (O'Reilly, Sebastopol, Jan 1999)
32. L. Torvalds, Linux version 0.01 (1991), http://ftp.funet.fi/pub/linux/historical/kernel/old-versions/RELNOTES-0.01, Aug 1991

33. P. Tourani, B. Adams, A. Serebrenik, Code of conduct in open source projects, in *2017 IEEE 24th International Conference on Software Analysis, Evolution and Reengineering (SANER)* (2017), pp. 24–33
34. A. Vance, The defenders of free software. The New York Times (2010), http://www.nytimes.com/2010/09/26/business/26ping.html, Sept 25 2010
35. H. Yamagata, The Pragmatist of Free Software: Linus Torvalds Interview. Tokyo Linux Users Group (1997)

Chapter 5
Open-Source License Compliance in Software Supply Chains

Dirk Riehle and Nikolay Harutyunyan

Abstract Almost all software products today include open-source components. However, the obligations that open-source licenses put on their users can be difficult or undesirable to comply with [14, 20, 25]. As a consequence, software vendors and related companies need to govern the process by which open-source components are included in their products [7, 21]. A key process of such open-source governance is license clearance, that is, the process by which a company decides whether a particular component's license is acceptable for use in its products [4, 15, 19]. In this article, we discuss this process, review the challenges it poses to software vendors, and provide unanswered research questions that result from it.

5.1 License Compliance

A legally[1] valid software product complies with the licenses of all the open-source components included in the product [19]. An open-source license provides rights such as free (as in cost) use of the software in exchange for the fulfillment of obligations [14, 21]. Failure to meet these obligations leads to a legally invalid product. Some of these obligations could lead to intellectual property (IP) loss for the software vendor [14, 18, 20, 25].

---

[1] This article is a follow-up to the NII Shonan Meeting on "Towards Engineering Free/Libre Open Source Software (FLOSS) Ecosystems for Impact and Sustainability" where the first author was tasked with summarizing research questions in the domain of open-source license clearance and software supply chain management.

D. Riehle (✉) · N. Harutyunyan
Friedrich-Alexander Universität Erlangen-Nürnberg, Erlangen, Germany
e-mail: dirk@riehle.org
URL: http://osr.cs.fau.de

N. Harutyunyan
e-mail: nikolay.harutyunyan@fau.de

© Springer Nature Singapore Pte Ltd. 2019
B. Fitzgerald et al. (eds.), *Towards Engineering Free/Libre Open Source Software (FLOSS) Ecosystems for Impact and Sustainability*,
https://doi.org/10.1007/978-981-13-7099-1_5

5.1.1 License Obligations

Consider the following three example obligations [7, 18]:

- *License file provision.* The most common obligation is to provide the license file of each open-source component that comes with the product.
- *Copyright notice provision.* Another common obligation is to provide all copyright notices from all files of each open-source component.
- *Offer to provide source code (Copyleft[2]).* The Copyleft obligation is to either provide the product source code outright or to make a written offer to provide it upon request.

Some obligations are easy to comply with and some are not. Some obligations are unproblematic and some are highly undesirable from the intellectual property (IP) perspective of the vendor [13, 17, 25].

We therefore classify license obligations into three main types as follows:

- *Unproblematic* (easy to comply with and unproblematic from an IP perspective). An example is the license file provision.
- *Difficult-to-comply-with* (difficult to comply with, but unproblematic from an IP perspective). An example is the complete copyright notice provision.
- *Undesirable* (from an IP perspective). For many, but not all, business models, an example is the obligation to provide source code outright or to offer to provide the source code.

5.1.1.1 Potentially Difficult-to-Comply-with License Obligations

Whether an obligation is easy to comply with or not depends on various issues. For example, with improved tools, some obligations that are difficult to comply with today may become easy to comply with in the future.

Consider the case of the obligation to provide all copyright notices from all files of the original open-source code. In theory, if all files were available and with adequate tool support, it would be possible to compile a document with all copyright notices.

However, this is based on the premise that the origin of every line of source code is known and has been documented. There is no guarantee for this. Developers easily and often copy code from the web and may have pasted code from one component into another without properly documenting it. Without such documentation, it is nearly impossible to determine the original source and therefore nearly impossible to comply with its license obligations.

---

[2]Free Software Foundation, What Is Copyleft? at https://www.gnu.org/licenses/copyleft.en.html.

5.1.1.2 Potentially Undesirable License Obligations

Whether a particular obligation is undesirable from the perspective of a vendor depends on the vendor's intellectual property strategy, which in turn depends on its business model. A traditional closed-source vendor, for example, deriving significant revenue from license fees, may not want to be forced to license out their IP because of a Copyleft obligation [1].

Examples of license obligations often considered undesirable are as follows:

- *Written offer to provide source code (Copyleft).* If this clause triggers, the vendor has to provide the source code outright or to provide the source code upon request under the Copyleft license [3, 13], thereby losing exclusive usage rights, among other downsides.
- *Patent retaliation clause.* This clause, if triggered, usually withdraws the right to use the open-source component or the patent or both and thereby renders the product legally invalid, if the vendor enforces patent rights against someone else (the specifics depend on the license).
- *Lack of patent grant.* Some older licenses do not include a patent grant [17, 28]. Thus, any use of the open-source component in a product exposes the vendor to a potential patent enforcement action by a patent holder who contributed an implementation of the patent to the open-source component.

A firm that is earning its living by providing services and support for open-source components may not worry about Copyleft but rather develop all software in the open. Depending on the warranties and indemnification the firm provides to its customers, however, it may worry about other issues like lack of patent grants.

5.1.2 License Strategy

A rational software vendor can only accept components with unproblematic licenses into their products.

If the vendor were to accept a difficult-to-comply-with license, it might not be able to comply with the obligations and therefore end up with a legally invalid product. This opens the door for the original copyright holders to sue the vendor for license violation [1]. The Software Freedom Conservancy, a not-for-profit foundation, funds such lawsuits with the goal of enforcing license compliance. Also, developers exist, who pursue such a strategy for personal enrichment [19]; the details of the legal strategies are not of concern here.

If the vendor were to accept an undesirable obligation, the vendor might face a situation in which recipients of the software product insist on the vendor complying with the obligation. The vendor might decide to comply and face the consequences, for example, loss of exclusive rights to the intellectual property it created, or the vendor might decide to fight the request in court, leading to legal costs, lost management attention, and loss of reputation, among other downsides [19].

As a consequence, a software vendor needs to make sure that only open-source components with unproblematic licenses are used in a product. This specific process of clearing a suggested open-source component for use in a product is the license clearance process [4, 15, 19]. License clearance is part of open-source governance, which is part of overall product governance.

5.2 Product Governance

Product governance is the governance of all involved parties, their roles, and responsibilities, as well as their processes and practices over the course of the product's life. It is mostly a product management task, but also involves engineering management and software architecture. Open-source governance is that part of product governance that is concerned with the use of, contribution to, and leadership of open-source software projects as they are relevant to the vendor's product.

Open-source license clearance is one process of open-source governance, and the main concern of this article. However, to understand license clearance, we first need to understand the complexity of software products and how open-source software makes it into a product.

5.2.1 Product Architecture

Software products and most software components are built from other software components. As a consequence, a software product can be viewed as a graph of interconnected software components and fragments. The properties of the constituent parts of a product and their relationships are all relevant to product governance and need to be modeled precisely. Capturing this information is a precondition for achieving license compliance [8, 9], that is, correctly fulfilling all the obligations that the use of open-source components puts onto the software vendor.

5.2.1.1 The Component Graph

Figure 5.1 illustrates the architecture of a product as a code component graph. The final product is shown at the top, and it depends on (incorporates and uses) various other components. These other components may have been developed by the vendor or they may have been sourced from a third party. Closed-source vendors and open-source projects are both viable sources of third-party components.

Example properties of interest for a given code component include the following:

- *its license(s),*
- *any known vulnerabilities, or*

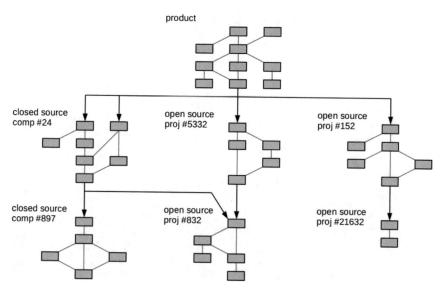

Fig. 5.1 The architecture of an example product from the code component perspective

- *its export restrictions [22], for example, due to cryptography algorithms.*

An important view of the code architecture is management domains, which cluster components by their managers, that is, closed-source vendors or open-source project communities. A management domain corresponds with the traditional notion of a (possibly multicomponent) third-party code component. Typically, but not always, those who manage such a domain also own the copyright.

Figure 5.2 illustrates these management domains. Components of the same management domain usually, but not necessarily, have the same license. For example, the OpenJDK project, delivers many components, but most importantly the core runtime library needed by any Java application. This large library aggregates many other components of varying but compatible open-source licenses.

5.2.1.2 Component Relationships

Viewing a product's code architecture as a graph of interdependent components requires engineering managers, software architects, and developers to be clear not only about which components to use (the nodes) but also to be clear as to how they relate (the edges). This is particularly important, if the component relationship crosses from one domain into another. From a license compliance perspective, understanding the component and fragment relationships is critical to making good decisions during the license clearance process. Depending on the type of relationship, license obligations may or may not apply [5].

Examples of relationship types are as follows:

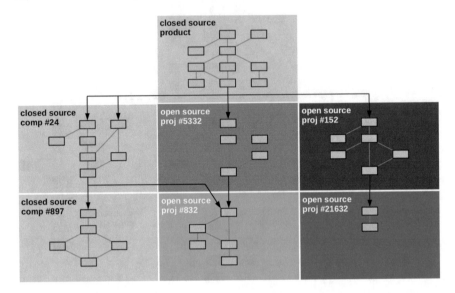

Fig. 5.2 The code architecture of Fig. 5.1 scoped by management domains

- *the statically imported library,*
- *the dynamically loaded library, and*
- *the web services call.*

Also, copying code from the web or other places and pasting it into a software component introduces a dependency of the component onto some other party's intellectual property. Search engines, discussion forums, and question–answer websites for programmers make copying and pasting code easy today and it constitutes a frequent occurrence. Product governance policies may prevent this for closed-source code, but open-source projects typically do not have such provisions in place.

5.2.1.3   Code Architecture Model

Traditional modeling tools for software architecture do not support management domain views of code component architectures. Such a view, however, is often provided by tool vendors specializing in license compliance.

Still, most vendors, if they track the code component architecture for license compliance purposes at all, maintain a spreadsheet with the components, their licenses, and other metadata. From this spreadsheet, the so-called bill of materials, license compliance artifacts like license texts, and copyright notice compilations can be generated.

In theory, any component could provide its metadata so that build tools could collect all relevant information and build the bill of materials automatically [9].

Sadly, this is not being done widely. As a consequence, most companies maintain a product's bill of materials by hand.

5.2.2 Make or Buy Decisions

From a software vendor's perspective, most components will be sourced from third parties, where third-party providers can be other companies or open-source projects. Free (as in cost) open-source software is a great value proposition for software startups, but even established software vendors benefit from the cost reduction of using high-quality components for free [2].

The main decision, whether to make or buy a particular software component for use as part of a product, is a product management decision. The driving criterion is whether the software component will in any way support the competitive differentiation of the product in the marketplace or not. If the component is not competitively differentiating, it should probably be sourced from a third party.

If no such component exists, the company may have to develop the component itself, but typically should do so as an open-source component to harness the benefits that an engaged open-source community can bring [10, 23, 24]. These benefits are as follows:

- *maturing the component faster,*
- *helping recruiting new and competent employees, and*
- *improving employee loyalty.*

5.2.3 The Software Supply Chain

Software vendors need to look at their product's code component architecture and their sourcing of not competitively differentiating components as a form of software supply chain management. They need to evaluate third parties as suppliers of components toward sustainability, quality, and costs, among other criteria.

Third-party suppliers can be commercial companies or open-source projects. Companies may be providing closed-source components or they may be providing open-source components with additional (to-pay-for) services like warranties or support.

The supply chain view of a code component architecture naturally leads to supplier tiers, with the first tier of suppliers having a direct relationship with the vendor, and tiers further removed having an indirect relationship with the vendor. Still, the actions of tier 2 or higher suppliers directly impact the vendor's product [26]. Figure 5.3 illustrates the tier-view of the code component architecture.

A direct relationship with a supplier allows a vendor to enforce their license strategy. For example, in a contract with a closed-source supplier, the vendor may be able

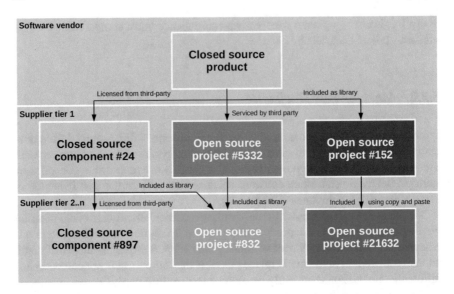

Fig. 5.3 The supply chain perspective of the code component architecture of an example product

to specify that only unproblematic open source be used. Or, when choosing an open-source component, the vendor may select only components with an unproblematic license.

However, contracts or declarations do not necessarily guarantee that reality conforms to them.

For example, a commercial supplier may promise, by contract, that no open source is used in their products. However, they may fail to enforce proper governance processes that ensure that developers do not copy open-source code or include open-source components in their components. Delivered as a binary, it may be difficult for the vendor to determine whether the supplier is meeting its contractual obligations.

Also, the declared license of an open-source component may not necessarily be the real license of the component. Developers may have copied code from elsewhere that forces a license change, but may have failed to declare it. Or, some licenses conflict with each other, leading to software that cannot be used legally [5]. While the source code is available for analysis, determining any such license violation or confusion is not trivial.

Tiers 2 and higher may present the same problems to their next lower tier, compounding the effect on the vendor as the final user of the software.

As a consequence, many lawyers believe that little legally valid software is left on the market. They assume that so much copying and pasting has taken place that all software has been tainted. Without knowing what is in their software, a vendor cannot be license compliant, and hence cannot ship a legally valid product.

The difficulty of determining unwanted code goes both ways: The vendor may find it difficult to determine, but so does the original copyright holder, who might have standing to sue. This mitigates the risks expressed through this otherwise bleak assessment.

5.2.4   Complete and Correct Bills of Materials

To be able to make an informed decision and to ensure license compliance, a vendor therefore needs to receive or develop a complete and correct bill of materials for a supplied component. Both industry and open-source communities have woken up to this challenge and are trying to address it.

The first step is to have a standard format for a bill of materials that expresses what is included in a component. For this, the Linux Foundation has sponsored the creation of the Software Package Data Exchange (SPDX) standard [27] and tools for processing the standard [19].

SPDX is rapidly evolving. SPDX compliant documents provide information about what is contained within a software package, including the license information of a contained component, who created the component, its version, etc.

A bill of materials also needs to be complete and correct. To this end, any open-source project needs to exercise good open-source governance. Guidelines of varying quality exist on the web [6, 12].

The Open Chain Project of the Linux Foundation is trying to address this problem by providing guidance to software vendors and open-source projects on how to have good open-source governance [16].

5.3   License Clearance

License clearance is short for license clearance process. It is the process of reviewing and deciding upon requests to include third-party components, in particular, open-source components, in products. Typically, this process is part of the overall open-source governance and compliance efforts of a company [7, 9, 14, 19, 25].

5.3.1   Process Preconditions

The license clearance process has to have, at a minimum, the following three key components [7, 19]:

- *A responsible person.* Someone needs to be tasked with the license clearance process. This person or post also needs to be known for being responsible for this process, and managers and developers need to have been educated to go to this person with any license clearance questions they may have.

- *A decision strategy.* The responsible person needs to know how to decide on a request to include an open-source component in a vendor's product. For this, they need the license strategy and all necessary expertise. They may have to work with additional experts, for example, the vendor's legal counsel.
- *Escalation powers.* Finally, the responsible person needs the power to enforce its decisions, typically by escalating a denied inclusion request that is getting ignored through the legal department to higher managerial levels in the company.

Vendors with state-of-the-art processes typically will have established some sort of open-source program office or open-source competence center, whose responsibilities include open-source governance, and hence the license clearance process [7, 11, 19].

5.3.2   The Clearance Process

The clearance process itself can get complicated, but does not have to. We have identified the following common best practices (in no particular order):

- *Blacklists and white lists.* With some licenses, the decision can be made quickly and independently of context. For example, the AGPLv3 license is typically not acceptable and should be blacklisted, while the Apache License 2.0 is typically unproblematic and can be white listed [9, 19].
- *Planned integration in products.* Sometimes, the context determines whether a particular component can be used. Depending on the embedding of the component in the product, unwanted obligations may not apply, in case of which the use of the component is unproblematic [5, 9].
  To make this decision, a model of the product architecture, as described in the previous section, is needed. A software architect needs to maintain the model to demonstrate to the license clearance process owner that the desired use of a component is unproblematic.
- *Review of license conflicts.* Some licenses conflict with each other, and hence the components of these licenses cannot be used in the same product [5]. Using the model of the product architecture that we introduced, the process owner can check for such conflicts.
- *Component repository.* For efficiency reasons, the vendor may maintain an internal repository of component versions that have previously been accepted for inclusion in products. This is an advanced form of white listing, making the use of open-source components a self-service process.
  Since security vulnerabilities may not be known at the time of including a component in the repository, all white-listed components need to be monitored for newly discovered vulnerabilities and reevaluated in the light of any new information.
  A side effect of providing a component repository is enhanced security. Developers should use components from the internal repository rather than a public one, reducing the attack surface for anyone trying to harm the vendor's products.

- *Component tracking.* Components in products need to be tracked. The first step is to maintain the product architecture model. The second step is to continuously review new information about the components embedded in the vendor's products.

New information may be problems with the license, new known vulnerabilities, or increased legal activities for the component. The vendor needs to react to such information, for example, by removing a component or upgrading the product to a new version of the component.

5.4 Research Questions

The base of any license clearance is a complete and correct product architecture model. To build this model, the following challenges need to be mastered:

- How to receive a complete and correct bill of materials for an open-source component?
  - How to represent this bill of material?
  - How to automatically generate the bill of material from project artifacts?
  - How to identify post-facto that code has been copied into a component from elsewhere?
- How to motivate an open-source project community to clean up its code?
  - How to motivate an open-source project community to create a bill of material?
  - How to motivate an open-source project community to apply good open-source governance?
- How to represent and work effectively with the product architecture model?
  - How to automatically generate complete and correct license compliance artifacts?

With a complete and correct product architecture model in place, the following challenges can be addressed:

- How to determine whether a particular license combination is legally valid?
  - How to completely and correctly model license obligations and their combination?

Finally, the vendor faces the challenge of ensuring the model conforms to the source code, which is summarized below:

- How to ensure developers follow a proper license clearance process?
  - How to make the license clearance process known and understood?
  - How to ensure developers take the license clearance process serious?
  - How to make the license clearance process effective and not a burden?

Acknowledgements We would like to thank our colleagues Daniel German and Matti Rossi for the discussions and collaboration at the 2017 workshop on FLOSS ecosystems at Shonan Village, Japan. We also would like to thank Maximilian Capraro, Shane Coughlan, Michael Dorner, Monika Schnizer, and Axel Teichert for their feedback on this article.

References

1. B.W. Carver, Share and share alike: understanding and enforcing open source and free software licenses. Berkeley Technol. Law J. 443–481 (2005)
2. B. Fitzgerald, The transformation of open source software. MIS Q. 587–598 (2006)
3. Free Software Foundation (2007). GNU General Public License: Version 3, 2007, at http://www.gnu.org/licenses/gpl.html
4. D. German, M. Di Penta, A method for open source license compliance of java applications. IEEE Softw. **29**(3), 58–63 (2012)
5. D.M. German, A.E. Hassan, License integration patterns: addressing license mismatches in component-based development. in *Proceedings of the 31st International Conference on Software Engineering*. IEEE Computer Society (2009), pp. 188–198
6. GitHub (2017). Open source guides at https://opensource.guide/
7. I. Haddad, *Open Source Compliance in the Enterprise* (The Linux Foundation, San Francisco, 2016)
8. M. Helmreich, D. Riehle, Geschäftsrisiken und Governance von Open-Source in Softwareprodukten, in *Praxis der Wirtschaftsinformatik (HMD 283)*, 49. Jahrgang (2012), pp. 17–25
9. A. Hemel, S. Coughlan, *Practical GPL Compliance* (Linux Foundation, San Francisco, 2017), pp. 43–47
10. J. Henkel, Open source software from commercial firms–tools, complements, and collective invention. Z. Für Betr.Swirtschaft **4**, 1–23 (2004)
11. Hewlett-Packard Development Company L.P. (2007). Best practices in open source governance. White paper
12. C. Jensen, W. Scacchi, Governance in open source software development projects: a comparative multi-level analysis. *Open Source Software: New Horizons* (2010) pp. 130–142
13. D.M. Kennedy, A primer on open source licensing legal issues: copyright, copyleft and copyfuture. Louis Univ. Public Law Rev. **20**, 345 (2001)
14. A.M.S. Laurent, *Understanding Open Source and Free Software Licensing: Guide to Navigating Licensing Issues in Existing & New Software.* (O'Reilly Media Inc, Sebastopol, 2004)
15. C. Link, Patterns for the commercial use of open source: legal and licensing aspects, in *Proceedings of the 15th European Conference on Pattern Languages of Programs*, ACM, (2010), p. 7
16. Linux Foundation (2017). The open chain project at https://www.openchainproject.org/
17. R.J. Mann, The commercialization of open source software: do property rights still matter?. The University of Texas School of Law. Law and Economics Research Paper No. 58 (2005)
18. D. McGowan, Legal implications of open-source software. U. Ill. L. Rev. 241 (2001)
19. H.J. Meeker, *Open (Source) for Business: A Practical Guide to Open Source Software Licensing,* 2nd ed. (CreateSpace Independent Publishing Platform, Scotts Valley, 2017)
20. H.J. Meeker, The open source alternative: understanding risks and leveraging opportunities. (Wiley, New York, 2008)
21. C.H. Nadan, Open source licensing: virus or virtue. Tex. Intellect. Prop. Law J. **10**, 349 (2001)
22. H.E. Pearson, Open source licenses: Open source—the death of proprietary systems?. Comput. Law Secur. Rev. **16**(3), 151–156 (2000)
23. D. Riehle, The commercial open source business model. *Value Creation in E-Business Management* (2009), pp. 18–30

24. D. Riehle, The economic motivation of open source software: stakeholder perspectives. Computer **40**(4) (2007)
25. C. Ruffin, C. Ebert, Using open source software in product development: a primer. IEEE Softw. **21**(1), 82–86 (2004)
26. H. Schöttle, U. Steger, Managing open source software in the corporate environment. Comput. Law Rev. Int. **16**(1), 1–7 (2015)
27. K. Stewart, P. Odence, E. Rockett, Software package data exchange (SPDX) specification. Int. Free. Open Source Softw. Law Rev. **2**(2), 191–196 (2011)
28. S. Zhu, Patent rights under FOSS licensing schemes. Shidler J. Law Commer. Technol. **4**, 4–13 (2007)

Chapter 6
The Life and Death of Software Ecosystems

Raula Gaikovina Kula and Gregorio Robles

Abstract Software ecosystems have gained a lot of attention in recent times. Industry and developers gather around technologies and collaborate to their advancement; when the boundaries of such an effort go beyond certain amount of projects, we are witnessing the appearance of Free/Libre and Open Source Software (FLOSS) ecosystems. In this chapter, we explore two aspects that contribute to a *healthy* ecosystem, related to the attraction (and detraction) and the death of ecosystems. To function and survive, ecosystems need to attract people, get them onboarded, and retain them. In Section One, we explore possibilities with provocative research questions for attracting and detracting contributors (and users): the lifeblood of FLOSS ecosystems. Then, in the Section Two, we focus on the death of systems, exploring some presumed to be dead systems and their state in the afterlife.

6.1 Attractors (and Detractors) to FLOSS Projects

A contributing component to the sustainability (i.e., life) of a FLOSS project is its ability to attract new development. Although keeping current contributors is equally important, projects risk failure if they are unable to attract a healthy amount of new developers to provide rejuvenation and aid in project evolution, especially in response to ever-changing external forces (i.e., impactful events, new technologies, vulnerabilities, and rivals) that affect FLOSS projects. In this section, we discuss (1) the different forces of attraction (and detraction) that influence contributors to participate in specific projects, (2) the effect of these forces at the ecosystem level, and

---

Raula is the main contributor of attractors and detractors (i.e., life) to FLOSS Projects
Gregorio is the main contributor for the death of ecosystems

R. G. Kula (✉)
Nara Institute of Science and Technology, Ikoma, Japan
e-mail: raula-k@is.naist.jp

G. Robles
Universidad Rey Juan Carlos, Móstoles, Spain
e-mail: grex@gsyc.urjc.es

© Springer Nature Singapore Pte Ltd. 2019
B. Fitzgerald et al. (eds.), *Towards Engineering Free/Libre Open Source Software (FLOSS) Ecosystems for Impact and Sustainability*,
https://doi.org/10.1007/978-981-13-7099-1_6

finally present (3) three provocative research questions to further our understanding of attracting contributors to a project.

6.1.1   Forces of Attraction (and Detraction)

We classify known forces of attraction as either motivation related, environmental, or a combination of the two. Internal project-driven campaigns usually revolve around marketing strategies to attract developers. A study by Storey et al. [7] showed that communities of FLOSS projects are shaped through social and communication channels (sometimes referred to as social coding). Recently, Aniche et al. [2] confirmed that news channels also play an important role in shaping and sharing knowledge among developers. Hence, owners of projects could boost their social presence through participation on recent topics from news aggregators such as reddit,[1] Hacker News[2] and slashdot.[3] For instance, a project may employ new or well-known or recognizable trademarks that are trending in the news. Social media outlets and other communication channels can be leveraged to improve project attractiveness (i.e., innovative posts on Q&A forums such as StackOverflow[4] and social media endorsements and collaborations through twitter or facebook). Recently, analytical indicators of project health or fitness are aimed at increasing the appeal of a project. In detail, the emergence of online collaboration platforms GitHub, GitLab, and BitBucket, with specific features such as pull requests, forks, and stars depict the fitness of a project.

Other motivations are driven by external forces. Hata et al. [5] used game theory to identify three strategies that is likely to incite contributions. The authors suggest that improving the code writing mechanisms (i.e., wikis, official webpage, contributing and coding guidelines, and using multi-language formats). Second, in terms of monetary incentives, sites such as bountysource website[5] allow developers to be hired as bounty hunters to fix specialized bugs in a project. Finally, the impact of innovations such as social coding, introduced by online collaborations of GitHub has attracted attention of developers. A lesser explicit form of motivations is driven by a third party with their own interests. For instance, a company may allocate employees or provide monetary incentives to support (i.e., keep alive) a project of interest. This is especially in cases where a third party is interested in stimulating further feature development of an existing product that they are invested in.

Failing projects provide insights into some environmental forces that detract developers from making contributions. A study by Coelho and Valente [3] found the following reasons for failing projects: usurped by competitor, obsolete project, lack

---

[1]https://www.reddit.com.

[2]https://news.ycombinator.com.

[3]https://slashdot.org.

[4]https://stackoverflow.com.

[5]https://www.bountysource.com/.

of time and interest, outdated technologies, low maintainability, conflicts among developers, legal problems, and acquisition. To mitigate these detractors, the authors propose three strategies to rejuvenate contributions in failing FLOSS projects. First, projects are encouraged to improve their stability by *moving toward an organization account instead of a personal account*. Second, failing projects are encouraged to *transfer the project to new maintainers*. This is especially needed if the current maintainers' activity has been deteriorating over time. Finally, the project is encouraged to *accept new core developers*. This organizational factor aims to rejuvenate and ignite fresh ideas, giving new life to the project.

6.1.2   Forces at the Ecosystem Level

To date, existing works performed their analysis in respect to individual projects. At a higher level of abstraction, there exists cases where the forces of attraction (and detractions) in several projects in an ecosystem are triggered by a common event. For instance, several studies [1, 4, 6] investigated the eventful case of the JavaScript "left-pad" incident (see [8]), where removal of a trivial library package caused major breakages in thousands of projects including notable JavaScript frameworks like babel and react.

Other examples of impactful events at the ecosystem level include responses to wide-spreading high-risk security vulnerabilities (i.e., ShellShock, Heartbleed, and Poodle), rivaling technologies (i.e., battles between competing frameworks for specific programming domains such as PHP[6] and JavaScript[7]) and inadequacies in the current situation. As an example, current inadequacies could be realized when a change in management occurs (i.e., such as change of the middleman in InnerSource[8]). Changes in management (i.e., especially the single movement of a key contributor) may set off a chain series of attract and distraction forces that leave behind a rippling effect across the ecosystem. We theorize that these forces impact ecosystem sustainability, especially if affected projects act as hubs within that ecosystem.

---

[6]A blog post for 2018 best PHP frameworks at https://coderseye.com/best-php-frameworks-for-web-developers/.

[7]A blog that shows the trend changes between rival JavaScript frameworkshttps://stackoverflow.blog/2018/01/11/brutal-lifecycle-javascript-frameworks/.

[8]InnerSource takes the lessons learned from developing FLOSS and applies them to the way companies develop software internally. Taken from https://paypal.github.io/InnerSourceCommons/.

6.1.3   Provocative Research Questions

To conclude this section, we formulate a set of provocative research questions to further our understanding of attraction and detraction forces:

- **What are the strengths and successes of known attractor strategies to FLOSS projects?** We have identified many attraction forces. Understanding the strength and success of these different attractors will assist us to treat projects that may be suffering with attracting new contributors to their projects.
- **How often are these attractor strategies practiced in the real world and in respect to different ecosystems?** It is unknown to what extent and the frequency by which these strategies are practiced by practitioners in recent times. Furthermore, we are unclear of the environmental and ecosystem conditions required to sustain these attraction forces.
- **What are the implications and impact of these forces of attraction at the ecosystem level?** We theorize that attraction forces may impact the overall ecosystem. However, it is unclear the extent by which these forces of attraction may affect the sustainability of the overall ecosystem itself.

6.2   On the Death of Ecosystems

Software ecosystems have gained a lot of attention in recent times. Industry and developers gather around technologies and collaborate to their advancement; when the boundaries of such efforts go beyond certain amount of projects, we are witnessing the appearance of a software ecosystem. Software ecosystems are complex in nature, as many stakeholders are involved. There are for sure key people (e.g., Guido van Rossum in Python) and projects (such as MySQL in the MySQL ecosystem), but activity follows a decentralized pattern, more in the fashion of stigmergic process as known, for instance, from colonies of ants.

In this section, we want to focus on the death of software ecosystems. While it is known that many FLOSS projects are discontinued, to the knowledge of the authors we have not found any research on the topic of software ecosystems. We define as the death of a project as having no activity in it for a long period as done in other research works. So, a dead software ecosystems have would have no activity. It should be noted that other definitions of death could be proposed. One may think of having no users, a loss of interest in the software industry, a decrease in developers, developer interest, etc.

On the other hand, we are not looking after projects, which are defined (i.e., they have a goal) and concrete software solution that has an organizational and logistic structure (a known website, repository, mailing list, etc.). Software ecosystems are built of many projects, which coordinate themselves (or not) but that have a relationship that is in general technological (although other types of ecosystems such as the (entire) Apache ecosystem orchestrates around collaboration).

6.2.1   *Research Questions*

Current research literature has so far focused mainly on successful FLOSS systems, to see how they are articulated and organized, in order to derive lessons learned out of these. Our method will be exploratory and based on case studies. Specifically, we want to address following RQs:

- **RQ₁. What do we know of dead ecosystems?**
  We want to approach our study based on real cases of ecosystems that were so in the past, but that are now inactive. So, as a first step, we performed an unstructured search for dead ecosystems, by asking participants in the workshop and then by looking in the web (mainly in the webpages of its projects and in Wikipedia) for more information. The output of this research question is a list of dead ecosystems on which the subsequent RQs will be addressed.
- **RQ₂. Why are these ecosystems dead?**
  Once we have identified dead ecosystems in RQ1, we would like to dig into the reasons why these have become inactive. In this regard, we would like to see if the cause of the inactivity can be technology (e.g., becoming an outdated technology), economic (e.g., failure of funding), legal (i.e., patent or license issues), among others. As input of information, we will use Google searches on the Internet.
- **RQ₃. What can we learn from dead ecosystems?**
  Once we have identified dead ecosystems (RQ1) and have further information into what causes are behind its death (RQ2), our goal is to see if we can extract major insight into the topic. The final goal is, of course, to help software ecosystems to stay "healthy".

6.2.2   *Findings*

Based on research questions in the prior section, in this section, we discuss and present the findings of each research question.

6.2.2.1   *RQ₁* **What Do We Know of Dead Ecosystems?**

During the seminar in Shonan, participants were asked informally regarding open ecosystems that have been discontinued. After much discussion, as shown in Table 6.1, the following dead systems arose from the discussions.

Control Versioning System (CVS)

CVS is a version control system, an important component of Source Configuration Management (SCM).[9] Using it, you can record the history of sources files and docu-

---

[9] Website is at https://www.nongnu.org/cvs/.

Table 6.1 Summary of the studied dead ecosystems

System name	Brief description	Discontinued date
Concurrent Versioning System (CVS)	version control	May, 2008
FireFoxOS	mobile operating system	Dec, 2015
Apache Geronimo	application server	May, 2013
Maemo	mobile development platform	Feb, 2010

ments. The last version of CVS was published in 2008 (see http://savannah.nongnu. org/news/?group=cvs).

FirefoxOS

Firefox OS was a mobile operating system, based on HTML5 and the Linux kernel, available for several platforms. It was developed by Mozilla Corporation under the support of other companies and a large community of volunteers from around the world. The operating system was designed to allow HTML5 applications to communicate directly with device hardware using JavaScript and Open Web APIs.[10]

In December 2015, Mozilla announced it would stop development of new Firefox OS smartphones and in September 2016 announced the end of development.

Apache Geronimo

Apache Geronimo[11] is a FLOSS application server developed by the Apache Software Foundation and distributed under the Apache license. IBM announced on May 14, 2013 that it would withdraw and discontinue support of Apache Geronimo (see http://www-01.ibm.com/common/ssi/rep_ca/1/897/ENUS913-081/ENUS913-081.PDF). This was also communicated through their website and mailing lists.

Maemo

Maemo[12] is a development platform for handheld devices based on debian GNU / Linux. Maemo is mostly based on open-source code and has been developed by Maemo Devices within Nokia in collaboration with many FLOSS projects such as the Linux kernel, Debian, and GNOME.

At the Mobile World Congress 2010, Intel and Nokia announced that they would unite their Linux-based platforms into a single product called MeeGo. The Linux Foundation canceled MeeGo in September 2011 in favor of Tizen. An emerging Finnish company, Jolla, took Mer, a successor based on the MeeGo community, and created a new operating system: Sailfish OS, and launched a new smartphone at the end of 2013.

---

[10] Although an official website is not found, the blog of one of the key engineers is an example of its existence https://medium.com/@bfrancis/the-story-of-firefox-os-cb5bf796e8fb.

[11] Website available at http://geronimo.apache.org/.

[12] Website available at http://maemo.org/intro/.

Table 6.2   Emergent projects after the death of the ecosystem

System name	Example emergent projects
Concurrent Versioning System (CVS)	CVSNT
FireFoxOS	Panasonic variant, H5OS, KaiOS, Jio
Apache Geronimo	Tomcat, EJB, Derby
Maemo	MeeGo, Tizan, Mer

6.2.2.2   *RQ₂* Why are these Ecosystems Dead?

We have investigated what happened to the projects presented in RQ_1, to see if there is any continuation. In this regard, we investigate whether or not the original project is still alive, and if there have been any forks (i.e., others have taken the source code base and have evolved the software independently). As shown in Table 6.2, new projects emerged in the aftermath of the dying ecosystem.

CVS

Although the CVS project was discontinued, we find that due to the development of the Microsoft Windows, Linux, Solaris, HPUX, I5os, and Mac OS X ports, evidence shows that CVS has split off into a separate project named CVSNT,[13] which is under current, active development (i.e., the latest update as of writing was April 2018).

FirefoxOS

After the discontinuation of Firefox OS, several variants of the OS have emerged. Panasonic will continue to develop the operating system for use in their Smart TVs, which runs My Home Screen, powered by the Firefox OS. Acadine Technologies has derived their H5OS from Firefox OS as well. Li Gong, the founder of the company, has overseen the development of Firefox OS while serving as president of the Mozilla Corporation. Alcatel OneTouch GO FLIP uses a fork called KaiOS.[14] In addition, in July 2017, it was reported that Indian telecom operator Jio would be launching new feature phone with OS derived from Firefox OS and the apps are purely in HTML5 and CSS.

Apache Geronimo

The development of Apache Geronimo ceased around 2013, after its 3.0.1 release, when IBM and Oracle stopped to support the project in favor of their own technologies. Geronimo is not a single technology, but is the sum of many components, like Apache Tomcat,[15] Apache EJB,[16] Apache Derby,[17] among others. Many of these

---

[13]Website available at https://www.march-hare.com/cvspro/.

[14]Website at https://www.kaiostech.com/.

[15]Website as http://tomcat.apache.org/.

[16]Website at http://tomee.apache.org/tomcat-ejb.html.

[17]Website at https://db.apache.org/derby/.

components are used in the implementation components of other frameworks as can be seen from http://arjan-tijms.omnifaces.org/2014/05/implementation-components -used-by.html.

Maemo

In February 2010, the Maemo project from Nokia merged with Moblin to create the MeeGo mobile software platform under the umbrella of the Linux Foundation. However, the Maemo community continued to be active in Maemo. That is the reason why Nokia transferred the Maemo ownership first to the Hildon Foundation, and then to a German association called Maemo Community e.V. The last general assembly of this association has been in October 2017.

MeeGo[18] was canceled in September 2011, although a community-driven successor called Mer[19] was formed that. A Finnish start-up, Jolla, chose in 2013 Mer as the basis of the Sailfish OS operating system for their Jolla Phone smartphones. Another Mer derivative called Nemo Mobile is also currently developed actively.

6.2.2.3 *RQ₃* What Can We Learn From Dead Ecosystems?

There is little to learn from dead ecosystems, because software ecosystems, at least those that are FLOSS, do not die! In our quest for dead ecosystems, what we have found are that ecosystems that have been abandoned have evolved (if not completely, at least partially) with a given name. This means that organizations and names are the ones that may disappear, but the technology can be found years later in other projects and developments. There are two main factors that may concur to explain this situation as follows:

1. **Forks originating from the dead ecosystem.** The first one is the right to fork that exists (and is used) in FLOSS development. Although forking (i.e., splitting the community by taking the technology under a new name) is historically not welcome in the FLOSS community, it is understood in certain contexts. One of these situations is when the project is abandoned.
2. **Technological advancements.** The second one is related to the development of technologies. This requires time, much human labor and is maintenance intensive. A software is not only its development and its community. It is as well the number of tests and maturity that it has achieved. Successful FLOSS ecosystems have invested a large amount of effort in becoming mature. Even if its key players lose their interest in the technology and the community seems to shrink, there is always the source code, that is, result of that effort. In addition, the investment in time and learning of other technologies results in inertia by those who are familiar with the technology. With ecosystems that have a large community, the probabilities of even a minor part of this community still interested in continuing with development is very high.

---

[18] A variant of MeeGo is Tizen https://www.tizen.org/.

[19] Website as http://www.merproject.org/.

6.2.3   Conclusions

FLOSS ecosystems are still too young to draw conclusions from our investigation, but as far as we have analyzed we have not found any (well-known) FLOSS ecosystem that can be considered dead (i.e., completely abandoned). For one or the other reason, the original software has evolved into other systems and communities and still serves, even if the importance of the project is not the one that used to be.

A lesson learned from our analysis is that if organizations want sustainability of a technology or application, they should strive for the ecosystem way. This is a lesson that could be of interest for consortia, public bodies, and companies wanting to set a standard. The network effects of developing a long-lasting software ecosystem are the probability that at least a small portion of the community keeps it alive. We have seen that this is the case from outdated technologies (like CVS) to hardware-linked software (such as Maemo).

As there is a growing interest of corporations in FLOSS, such as the one that can be found in OpenStack, OW2, WebKit, among others, we are sure that the future will allow to have further examples of ecosystems and analyze how they evolve, even when their main promoters abandon.

References

1. R. Abdalkareem, O. Nourry, S. Wehaibi, S. Mujahid, E. Shihab, Why do developers use trivial packages? an empirical case study on npm, in *Proceedings of the 11th Joint Meeting of the European Software Engineering Conference and the ACM SIGSOFT Symposium on the Foundations of Software Engineering (ESEC/FSE'17)* (2017)
2. M. Aniche, C. Treude, I. Steinmacher, I. Wiese, G. Pinto, M.A. Storey et al., How modern news aggregators help development communities shape and share knowledge, in *International Conference on Software Engineering (ICSE18)* (2018)
3. J. Coelho, M.T. Valente, Why modern open source projects fail, in *Proceedings of the 2017 11th Joint Meeting on Foundations of Software Engineering ESEC/FSE 2017* (ACM, New York, USA, 2017). pp. 186–196
4. A. Decan, T. Mens, M. Claes, An empirical comparison of dependency issues in OSS packaging ecosystems, in *2017 IEEE 24th International Conference on Sofware Analysis, Evolution and Reengineering (SANER)*, IEEE (2017). pp. 2–12
5. H. Hata, T. Todo, S. Onoue, K. Matsumoto, Characteristics of sustainable oss projects: a theoretical and empirical study. in *2015 IEEE/ACM 8th International Workshop on Cooperative and Human Aspects of Software Engineering* (2015). pp. 15–21
6. R. Kikas, G. Gousios, M. Dumas, D. Pfahl, Structure and evolution of package dependency networks. in *Proceedings of the 14th International Conference on Mining Software Repositories MSR '17* (IEEE Press, Piscataway, NJ, USA, 2017). pp. 102–112
7. M.A. Storey, A. Zagalsky, F.F. Filho, L. Singer, D.M. German, How social and communication channels shape and challenge a participatory culture in software development. IEEE Trans. Softw. Eng. **43**(2), 185–204 (2017). Feb
8. The npm Blog – kik, left-pad, and npm (2018), http://blog.npmjs.org/post/141577284765/kik-left-pad-and-npm. Accessed 31 Jan 2018

Chapter 7
Onboarding and Retaining of Contributors in FLOSS Ecosystem

Minghui Zhou

Abstract There is a saying that the type of developers that an ecosystem *wants* do not have trouble getting involved. They are good at finding tasks and issuing pull requests. The type of developers that needs hand-holding—you do not want them joining your project/ecosystem due to their lack of skill. This might be true for a popular project like the Linux kernel which never worried attracting new developers. The (difficult) process of working around to get (a patch) in for a contributor is a process of getting the right people for the community. However, many other projects/ecosystem, e.g., GNOME, do not have many people who desperately want to work for them. And they have many to-do tasks. Projects even as popular as the Linux kernel are often in the need of resources. Moreover, the tasks in an ecosystem are quite different, what if the community just wants people who are able to review English documents? We may be able to train them well with a good design. In summary, there might be something we could do to help people with willingness (and no right skills yet) to get to the right track needed by ecosystems.

7.1 Onboarding

7.1.1 Background

The start of participation in a FLOSS ecosystem is fraught with difficulties [23, 31], as the new contributors may not be familiar with project's practices and norms and the existing participants have to rely on the scant information in a bug report or a comment made by the newcomer to judge the competence and reliability of the

M. Zhou (✉)
Key Laboratory of High Confidence Software Technologies, Ministry of Education, Peking University, Beijing 100871, China
e-mail: zhmh@pku.edu.cn

© Springer Nature Singapore Pte Ltd. 2019
B. Fitzgerald et al. (eds.), *Towards Engineering Free/Libre Open Source Software (FLOSS) Ecosystems for Impact and Sustainability*,
https://doi.org/10.1007/978-981-13-7099-1_7

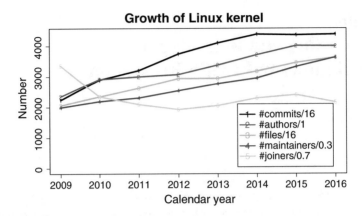

Fig. 7.1 Evolution of the Linux kernel over time

new contributor. Figure 7.1 shows the evolution of the Linux kernel over time.[1] In particular, the number of joiners decreases in recent years while the amount of work represented by files, commits, and authors which the community needs to take care of keeps growing. Getting a newbie on board in an ecosystem may be much more complicated than in a traditional project, because an ecosystem often has different projects and these projects often have interdependencies and require more learning. Moreover, the complexity of an ecosystem grows over time substantially, e.g., the Linux kernel has grown from 10.2 thousand lines of code in 1991 (version 0.01) to 22.3 million lines of code in 2016 (version 4.9), and from several authors to more than 2000 authors [27]. However, the nature of learning for individuals is the same, what differs may lie on the scale and content of learning.

The research questions which are critical to onboarding include the following:

1. How do newcomers learn? It involves what they need to learn and how to learn. For example, except the programming skills, they need to learn a methodology they did not invent and they need to learn how to communicate with the community. It also involves intermediaries (e.g., tools) that help to transfer knowledge and facilitate learning. How to learn? For example, learn by doing, or learn from experts or artifacts.
2. How do existing participants learn? The existing participants in the community are often busy with various tasks. Even if they want to spend effort on nurturing newcomers, they may not know what is needed for the newcomers due to the knowledge gap between them and newcomers—though they may naturally educate newcomers in the process of resolving problems (while newcomers learn by doing).

---

[1]The calculation is based on the data retrieved from the mainline repository of Linux kernel maintained by Linus Torvalds: http://www.git://git.kernel.org/pub/scm/linux/kernel/git/torvalds/linux.git.

3. What would be a good way to structure a community/ecosystem to get newcomers onboarding? For example, an often adopted policy is to have a division of modules and tasks. So newbies could focus their effort on easier modules or tasks—an often mentioned barrier faced by newcomers is that they do not know where to start.

These questions sketch an ecosystem-learning-focused agenda that needs to address the outlined challenges. Several important aspects that require extensive attention are discussed below.

7.1.2 Communication

The new developer population needs to learn the norms that enable them into the ecosystem. However, the culture of a long-lived ecosystem is difficult to understand. How to communicate with the community to acquire skills and knowledge that are needed to proceed in the ecosystem is a critical challenge in onboarding.

Newbies may acquire the skills and knowledge embodied in the community by directly interacting with master members (by reading their code and by asking them questions) [14]. The communication between newcomers and experts of a community is a two-way communication. On the one hand, newbies need to spend effort to learn basic norms and practices of the community by themselves (before asking questions); otherwise, the experts in the community may "get grumpy" because many simple mistakes are made over and over again, as described by one Linux kernel maintainer: "...you can answer a lot of questions like this for yourself very easily, simply by reading the source code."[2] As discovered by Steinmacher et al. [18], not needed pull requests are among the most common cause for code nonacceptance in FLOSS projects—because the newbies often submit "superseded/duplicated pull-requests".

On the other hand, experts may not be able to understand the confusion of newbies and may not communicate with them in an efficient way. There is a well-understood construct of the "zone of proximal development" [24], which describes the case where experts are not usually effective at training or teaching novices. The gap is too wide, the assumptions of what is known, too great. For example, Steinmacher et al. [17] found that one of the social barriers for people to contribute is "receiving answers with too advanced/complex contents." Therefore, people who are closer in experience level to newbies may be more effective at helping newbies learn practices. Due to the variation of new participants by nature, experts also need to learn how to communicate with different kinds of newbies.

In other words, for newcomers, it is important to understand how to do their homework and how to communicate with experts if necessary; and for experts, it is important to understand the (technical and social) needs of newcomers and make their nurturing effort worthwhile. Therefore, better communicating practices and mechanisms could be designed or adopted to help onboarding.

---

[2]https://github.com/gregkh/presentation-linuxmaintainer/blob/master/maintainer.pdf.

Moreover, experts inside the community may not have time to handle newbies. There is a need for intermediaries whose main purpose is to communicate with others. An idea of Social Mechanism of Interaction introduced by Schmidt et al., emphasizes the role of product itself in supporting the articulation of the distributed activities of multiple actors [15]. Not only codebase [6], but also bug report forms [3] are means by which the articulation work of the project, and therefore the communication can be carried out. Sometimes, the artifacts like MR/change repositories might be the only possible mechanism for developers to communicate [33], for example, in the offshoring or trans-generation scenarios (like a long-lived FLOSS system), since there may be no traditional opportunities to communicate in many situations, and a new generation of developers may be unable to communicate with original creators who have retired or died a long time ago.

To improve communication through these social mechanisms (and many others that are not discussed here), more investigations are needed, involving how and why these mechanisms work or do not work, particularly for newcomers, and what could be improved.

7.1.3 Division of Tasks and Modularization

Segregation of tasks at the architecture level is valuable to a community for a variety of reasons. The tasks that are core could be reserved for experts; it also enables a dispersion of less risky code tasks toward newer contributors which may help to facilitate the onboarding process. In particular, for ecosystems that have evolved for decades, the scale and complexity of the software system is way too complicated for a newbie to master, let alone to revise the code. However, if the tasks can be well divided, the newbies may be able to start from the easy tasks, e.g., ones that have no or few dependencies on the other parts of the system, and get on board quickly.

Though the tasks suitable for newbies have been rarely addressed explicitly, the division of labor and distribution of tasks is a common theme in the FLOSS literature. Researchers, e.g., Ducheneaut [7], characterized a community as a series of concentric circles; each circle is occupied by people playing a particular role in the development process. The core team accomplishes central tasks and oversees the community [1, 13, 27]. Peripheral roles, e.g., triagers, are found to be good at filtering invalid issues and as accurate as developers in filling in missing issue attributes [26]. These peripheral roles may suit newbies who are not familiar with code yet, as suggested by many FLOSS communities.

Modularization is adopted in software projects for the convenience of separating tasks. In particular, for a long-lived ecosystem, it is extremely difficult for any newcomer to join the development. A well-modularized architecture might help with that. For example, the key to the success of the Linux is its modularity according to its creator [20]. Inside the system, the combination of modules has a structured hierarchy of dependence relations, but modules entering at the same level of the system can be developed independently from each other [1]. Therefore, different modules could evolve according to its own nature and some parts that require minimal interaction with other developers may fit newbies. In the Linux kernel, after more than two decades of evolution, the core modules like mm (memory management) appear to have become mature and very few newbies could participate in the development [27]. The peripheral modules like drivers keep growing to satisfy various needs of hardware manufacturers. "In order to support many independent devices and therefore many independent authors, it is important to make the subsystem extensible, so each hardware device driver is implemented as a separate (sub-)module that supports a common interface."[3] As a result, the tasks of driver development are often considered to represent lower entry barrier for newcomers.[4] However, modularization is often aspirational, and different projects and organizations are in different points along this continuum. This could be examined from existing software repositories and build processes.

In practice, a variety of FLOSS projects/ecosystems post the possible tasks they perceive that would be suitable for newbies to work on in the project page. For example, the Linux community has KernelNewbies which "is all about sharing knowledge and experience" for newbies.[5] Mozilla has a website called Bugs Ahoy that allows people to search through all of Mozilla's bug reports to find the ones that are most relevant to their areas of interest, for example, newbies could choose to display only "simple bugs".[6] Further investigation on how the roles are separated and how the tasks are distributed among the roles in large-scale FLOSS ecosystems are needed. It could certainly help onboarding in addition to many other benefits, for example, it helps to understand the governance of a community.

7.1.4 Learning of Experts

What is known about experts is important not because all learners are expected to become experts, but because the knowledge of expertise provides valuable insights into what the results of effective learning look like [2]. Understanding how experts learn and how they develop knowledge structure may provide ways to help newbies.

First, we need to understand the project/ecosystem practice trajectories that experts take. The issues include how a developer starts from a novice (a newcomer) and becomes an expert (a core team member), how she grows her expertise, and what kind of expertise she has to master (and in what order) to become central [29]. Some studies have been conducted about how the developers grow their strength in terms of task difficulty and task centrality [28], but much broader and deeper investigation is needed, for example, of what leads to that trajectory. Further, an ecosystem requires

---

[3]linux.org/threads/the-linux-kernel-the-source-code.4204/.

[4]https://www.linux.com/news/software/linux-kernel/804403-three-ways-for-beginners-to-contribute-to-the-linux-kernel/eudyptula-challenge.org.

[5]https://kernelnewbies.org/.

[6]https://www.joshmatthews.net/bugsahoy/?simple=1.

different kinds of participants who have different skills, it is important to separate their skills and trajectories (if it is possible) so people would know which trajectory to take based on their own preferences and skills.

Second, knowing how learners develop coherent structures of information has been particularly useful to understand the nature of organized knowledge that underlies effective comprehension and thinking. For example, the difference between seniors and novices, might lie in the ability to combine and apply what is learned to perform more complex activities creatively and in new situations [28]. Psychologists tried to aid software engineering through programmer selection testing since the 1950s. For example, McKeithan et al. [12] observed that experts are able to remember language commands based on their position in the structure of the language. Novices, not having an adequate mental representation of the language structure, often use mnemonic tricks to remember command names. Curtis [4] considered the performance of someone tackling a complicated programming task to be related to the richness of their knowledge about the problem area. However, the initial attempt had failed poorly, not because the principles and technologies of psychology were not up to the task, but because the psychologists failed to adequately model the mental and behavioral aspects of programming before selecting tests to measure it [4]. Learning theory can now account for how learners acquire skills to search a problem space and then use these general strategies in many problem-solving situations.

Overall, a better understanding of the programmer knowledge base, and why and how the programmer learn could help prepare newbies more efficiently. Different communities/organizations may have different cultures that suit how people get involved, empirical studies on existing ecosystems could benefit us in this regard.

7.2   Retaining

7.2.1   *Background*

It is critical for ecosystems to retain participants (who have become familiar with ecosystem practices and norms and have worked and established rapport with other participants), because people with multiyear participation in a project (or ecosystem at a higher level) tends to accomplish more and more important tasks, to provide greater value to the community than others, and are critical to the long-term viability of the community [16, 28, 30, 32]. While it is challenging to attract people, it is even more challenging to retain them. For example, Shah [16] found that a need for software-related improvements drives the initial participation, but only a small subset hobbyists remain involved. We found that only 3.6% of Gnome and 0.9% of Mozilla joiners would stay with the ecosystem for at least 3 years [32]. Figure 7.2 shows that the conversion of new joiners to long-term contributors who would stay with the

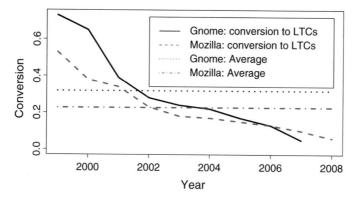

Fig. 7.2 Conversion of new joiners to long-term contributors (LTCs)

ecosystem for at least 3 years has been decreasing in Mozilla and GNOME.[7] It raises challenges that ecosystems must take seriously in order to survive and sustain.

The research questions which are critical to retaining include the following:

1. Why do people leave or stay?
2. What kind of people/expertise is needed (to stay long) by an ecosystem?
3. What could be designed in a community to retain contributors?

These questions motivate the following two important aspects that relate to retaining participants in an ecosystem.

7.2.2 Spectrum of Contributors

An ecosystem prospers with diverse contributions from diverse contributors. Ducheneaut [7] presented a pattern with core developers in the center, surrounded by the maintainers, often responsible for one or more subcomponents (modules) of a project. Around these are patchers (who fix bugs), bug reporters, documenters, and, finally, the users of the software.

In the spectrum of contributors, it is important for an ecosystem to know what kind of people it needs to retain, or what kind of people are needed to stay long for the survivability and sustainability of the ecosystem. This requires an understanding about the distribution of expertise needed in an ecosystem which is much more complicated than that of a single project due to the complicated dependencies between projects. For example, Wang et al. [25] proposed a novel view about the types of contributors needed in software development. They view software development as a combination of activities that require creation and activities that follow the routine

---

[7]The calculation is based on the data retrieved in [32].

manufacturing processes. Different activities call for different types of developers who need to be inspired and retained by different strategies.

Developer's expertise could be considered from various aspects. For example, the difficulty and centrality of tasks represent expertise or competence in a project/ecosystem, people who could accomplish central tasks are extremely valuable to sustain long-lived projects [28]. For example, Vasilescu et al. [21] showed that tenure diversity improves a team's productivity and turnover rate, which suggests that all levels of tenure are essential and what is critical might be how to keep a balance.

The spectrum of contributors required by an ecosystem could be explained through the media of people making contributions. The contributing media include mailing list, issue tracking system, version control system, question & answer websites, etc. These channels nurture different expertises required by an ecosystem in different ways. For example, the majority of the tasks of a senior QA in the issue tracking system of Mozilla is "going through the NEW/UNCONFIRMED pile of bugs contributed from outside sources (i.e., non-Netscape-paid employees)".[8] The responsibility of a maintainer in the Linux kernel is to "review patches from submitters (and then accept or reject it), handle questions from both developers and users about things related to the subsystem (usually bug reports)".[9] Both experienced QA and maintainers are critical to the sustainability of ecosystems but may require different skill sets, and therefore different methods to train and retain.

On the other hand, people come to join an ecosystem with different motivations and only a small fraction of them have the possibility to stay long. Some people would be simply one-time contributors, because they never attempt to stay no matter how attractive the ecosystem is. For example, some users run into problems when using Firefox, they may come to report the bugs (which are also important contributions for the software) and never come back. Some people may stay for long simply because that is their job. For example, in the Linux kernel some maintainers work for years maintaining drivers from companies such as Intel. Therefore, people who could be retained may occupy a small proportion of contributors. In order to understand how to retain them, this group of people needs to be located and carefully investigated. For example, the nature of the initial behavior of this group (e.g., the tasks they start may represent the motivation they have) and why they leave or stay.

7.2.3   Forces of Retaining

In order to sustain a community, it is important to understand what factors/ mechanisms might be at play to achieve that goal. The most influential factor to affect participation might be the motivation of a developer. In particular, FLOSS developers are likely to be motivated and involved in the project for fundamentally

---

[8]http://weblogs.mozillazine.org/stephend/.

[9]http://www.kroah.com/log/linux/what_greg_does.html.

different reasons. For example, Lakhani et al. [11] suggested that enjoyment-based intrinsic motivation is the strongest and most pervasive driver, with user need, intellectual stimulation derived from writing code, and improving programming skills being the top motivators for project participation (which may or may not suit sustaining). Nakakoji et al. [14] found that the willingness to get involved determines the role played by a FLOSS member in the community. We found that joiners who are more willing to contribute more than double their odds of becoming a long-term contributor [31].

The relationship between individuals and their environment might affect retention and have been extensively studied in the organizational literature. For example, the extent to which an individual's values are consistent with those revealed in his or her organization/environment was found to yield significant effects on a variety of attitudinal outcomes like job satisfaction and organizational commitment, and behavioral outcomes like job performance and turnover [8, 10, 22]. Similarly, in FLOSS projects, identity-based and bond-based commitments are found important for contributor retention [9]. If developers shared the beliefs and norms of the community, they engaged more in the effort related to the community [5, 19]. An ecosystem is combined with different cultures, the Linux Foundation, for example, does not have "a way" that all projects are compelled to follow, which makes retention even more challenging.

The macro-environment of an ecosystem, such as relatively sociality [30], user base (of the product), commercial support [27], and the popularity of the technology, has a substantial impact on the sustaining of contributors (and even the sustainability of the ecosystem itself). It is important to understand to what extent these factors play their roles and what is left for the community to tailor to retain valuable contributors.

Overall, the retention (or sustainability) of FLOSS participants is determined by a variety of factors, ranging from individual motivation to interaction between individuals and their environment. Further investigation may lie in the deeper understanding and quantification of the impact of various factors in large-scale ecosystems, and therefore helping to build mechanisms that could help retain participants.

Acknowledgements This work is supported by the National key research and development program Grant 2018YFB10044200, and the National Natural Science Foundation of China Grants 61432001 and 61825201.

References

1. C.R. Andrea Bonaccorsi, Why open source software can succeed. Res. Policy **32**, 1243–1258 (2003)
2. J. Bransford, A. Brown, R. Cocking, *How People Learn: Brain, Mind, Experience and School* (National Academy Press, Washington, 2003)
3. P. Carstensen, The bug report form (1994), http://cscw.dk/schmidt/papers/comic_d3.2.pdf
4. B. Curtis, Fifteen years of psychology in software engineering: individual differences & cognitive science, in *ICSE'84* (1984), pp. 97–106

5. S. Daniel, L. Maruping, M. Cataldo, J. Herbsleb, When cultures clash: participation in open source communities and its implications for organizational commitment, in *ICIS 2011 Proceedings* (7 Dec 2011), page Paper 7
6. C. de Souza, J. Froehlich, P. Dourish, Seeking the source: software source code as a social and technical artifact, in *GROUP '05: Proceedings of the 2005 International ACM SIGGROUP Conference on Supporting Group Work* (ACM, New York, USA, 2005), pp. 197–206
7. N. Ducheneaut, Socialization in an open source software community: a socio-technical analysis. Comput. Support. Coop. Work (CSCW) **14**(4), 323–368 (2005)
8. B.J. Hoffman, D.J. Woehr, A quantitative review of the relationship between person-organization fit and behavioral outcomes. J. Vocat. Behav. **68**(3), 389–399 (2006)
9. R.E. Kraut, P. Resnick, *Building Successful Online Communities: Evidence-Based Social Design* (MIT Press, Cambridge, 2012)
10. A.L. KRISTOF-BROWN, R.D. ZIMMERMAN, E.C. JOHNSON, Consequences of individuals' fit at work: a meta-analysis of person-job, person-organization, person-group, and person-supervisor fit. Pers. Psychol. **58**(2), 281–342 (2005)
11. K. Lakhani, R. Wolf, *Why Hackers Do What They Do: Understanding Motivation and Effort in Free/Open Source Software Projects* (MIT Press, Cambridge, 2005)
12. K. McKeithen, J. Reitman, H. Rueter, S. Hirtle, Knowledge organization and skill differences in computer programmers. Cogn. Psychol. **13**, 307–325 (1981)
13. A. Mockus, R.F. Fielding, J. Herbsleb, A case study of open source development: the Apache server, in *22nd International Conference on Software Engineering* (Limerick, Ireland, 4–11 June 2000), pp. 263–272
14. K. Nakakoji, Y. Yamamoto, Y. Nishinaka, K. Kishida, Y. Ye, Evolution patterns of open-source software systems and communities, in *IWPSE '02: Proceedings of the International Workshop on Principles of Software Evolution* (Orlando, FL, 19–20 May 2002), pp. 76–85
15. K. Schmidt, C. Simone, Coordination mechanisms: towards a conceptual foundation of CSCW systems design. J. Collab. Comput. **5**, 155–200 (1996)
16. S.K. Shah, Motivation, governance, and the viability of hybrid forms in open source software development. Manag. Sci. **52**(7), 1000–1014 (2006). July
17. I. Steinmacher, T. Conte, M.A. Gerosa, D. Redmiles, Social barriers faced by newcomers placing their first contribution in open source software projects, in *Proceedings of the 18th ACM Conference on Computer Supported Cooperative Work & Social Computing, CSCW '15* (ACM, New York, USA, 2015), pp. 1379–1392
18. I. Steinmacher, G. Pinto, I.S. Wiese, M.A. Gerosa, Almost there: a study on quasi-contributors in open source software projects, in *Proceedings of the 40th International Conference on Software Engineering, ICSE '18* (ACM, New York, USA, 2018), pp. 256–266
19. K.J. Stewart, S. Gosain, The impact of ideology on effectiveness in open source software development teams. MIS Q. **30**(2), 291–314 (2006)
20. L. Torvalds, The linux edge. Commun. ACM **42**(4), 38–39 (1999). Apr
21. B. Vasilescu, D. Posnett, B. Ray, M.G. van den Brand, A. Serebrenik, P. Devanbu, V. Filkov, Gender and tenure diversity in github teams, in *Proceedings of the 33rd Annual ACM Conference on Human Factors in Computing Systems* (ACM, 2015), pp. 3789–3798
22. M.L. Verquer, T.A. Beehr, S.H. Wagner, A meta-analysis of relations between person-organization fit and work attitudes. J. Vocat. Behav. **63**(3), 473–489 (2003)
23. G. von Krogh, S. Spaeth, K.R. Lakhani, Community, joining, and specialization in open source software innovation: a case study. Res. Policy **32**(7), 1217–1241 (2003). July
24. L. Vygotsky, Interaction between learning and development. Read. Dev. Child. **23**(3), 34–41 (1978)
25. H. Wang, G. Yin, X. Li, X. Li, *TRUSTIE: A Software Development Platform for Crowdsourcing* (Springer, Berlin, 2015)
26. J. Xie, M. Zhou, A. Mockus, Impact of triage: a study of mozilla and gnome, in *ESEM 2013* (Baltimore, Maryland, USA, 10–11 Oct 2013), pp. 247–250
27. M. Zhou, Q. Chen, A. Mockus, F. Wu, On the scalability of linux kernel maintainers' work, in *Proceedings of the 2017 11th Joint Meeting on Foundations of Software Engineering, ESEC/FSE 2017* (ACM, New York, USA, 2017), pp. 27–37

28. M. Zhou, A. Mockus, Developer fluency: achieving true mastery in software projects, in *ACM SIGSOFT / FSE* (Santa Fe, New Mexico, 7–11 Nov 2010), pp. 137–146
29. M. Zhou, A. Mockus, Growth of newcomer competence: challenges of globalization, in *FSE/SDP Workshop on the Future of Software Engineering Research* (Santa Fe, New Mexico, 7–8 Nov 2010), pp. 442–447
30. M. Zhou, A. Mockus, Does the initial environment impact the future of developers?, in *ICSE 2011* (Honolulu, Hawaii, 21–28 May 2011), pp. 271–280
31. M. Zhou, A. Mockus, What make long term contributors: willingness and opportunity in OSS community, in *ICSE 2012* (Zürich, Switzerland, 2012), pp. 518–528
32. M. Zhou, A. Mockus, Who will stay in the floss community? modeling participant's initial behavior. IEEE Trans. Softw. Eng. **41**(1), 82–99 (2015). Jan
33. M. Zhou, A. Mockus, D. Weiss, Learning in offshored and legacy software projects: how product structure shapes organization, in *ICSE Workshop on Socio-Technical Congruence* (Vancouver, Canada, 19 May 2009)

Chapter 8
A Free and Libre Open Source Software (FLOSS) Initiative for a Sustainable Deployment in Oman

Hadj Bourdoucen, Ahmed Al Maashri, Mohamed Ould-Khaoua, Mohamed Sarrab, Mahdi Amiri-Kordestani, Fahad Al Saidi and Khalil Al Maawali

Abstract Many countries worldwide are strongly encouraging and supporting the adoption of FLOSS in public and private sectors. This has fueled the rapid deployment of FLOSS solutions in numerous industrial sectors due to the benefits offered by FLOSS. These benefits include a high potential for job creation through local software customization, the growth of local SME's and IT skills, vendor lock-in prevention, improved security, and reduced licensing, installation and running costs. The trend was extending to other areas such as consumer associations, chamber of commerce, stock exchange, management associations, and nongovernmental organizations that are showing an increasing interest in many countries for FLOSS adoption. The Information Technology Authority (ITA) in Oman is the main enabler of FLOSS deployment in the public and private sectors. ITA has done considerable efforts in conjunction with a number of public and academic institutions, such as Sultan Qaboos University (SQU) and other higher educational institutions over the past few years in the FLOSS awareness, infrastructure, and capacity building fronts. However, to ensure the continuity and sustainability of the ongoing efforts, a roadmap for a sustainable FLOSS deployment for the public and private sectors is essential. The establishment of this roadmap for a sustainable deployment in the next 5 years was done based on an extensive study of the international FLOSS plans, the analysis of local FLOSS status in the public and private sectors through surveys and interviews, in addition to the views exchanged with a number of well-known international experts in the FLOSS community. Five deployment domains were identified in the

H. Bourdoucen (✉) · A. Al Maashri
Electrical and Computer Engineering Department, College of Engineering,
Sultan Qaboos University, Al Khod, P. O. Box 33, Muscat PC 123, Oman
e-mail: hadj@squ.edu.om

M. Sarrab · M. Amiri-Kordestani
CIRC, Sultan Qaboos University, Muscat, Oman

F. Al Saidi · K. Al Maawali
Information Technology Authority (ITA), Seeb, Oman

M. Ould-Khaoua
Department of Informatics, Saad Dahlab University, Blida, Algeria

© Springer Nature Singapore Pte Ltd. 2019
B. Fitzgerald et al. (eds.), *Towards Engineering Free/Libre Open Source
Software (FLOSS) Ecosystems for Impact and Sustainability*,
https://doi.org/10.1007/978-981-13-7099-1_8

roadmap with a number of initiatives for each domain that will be driven by a Center of Excellence (CoE) to assure the sustainability of the deployment. The CoE has a number of objectives to achieve; namely, transfer of technology, raising awareness on FLOSS in public and private sectors, promoting and implementing FLOSS solutions, formulating policies and guidelines, developing educational and training materials, conducting and supporting R&D in FLOSS, and working to optimize the overall cost of software licensing in Oman. Different models of this center were discussed and a realistic model was suggested for the implementation in Oman. It is proposed that the center should be funded by a Consortium of ministries.

8.1   Introduction

Many governments have policies that encourage FLOSS adoption. For instance, some policies mandate public agencies to use FLOSS software while others are in the process of forming general advice on preferable software. While proprietary software has its own international developers and supporters, adopting FLOSS motivates local IT companies to provide software services like technical support, training, customization, and development. In other words, adopting FLOSS often creates benefits for the local software industry, job creation (through entrepreneurship), capacity buildings, vendor lock-in, and localization for business culture and requirements. Such localization is beneficial for local capacity building sustainability and establishing a knowledge base grounded in indigenous resources that address local needs. Along with the benefits of localization are advantages that come from widening the scope for the creation and use of Arabic software. From an economic point of view, localization would expand the market for the country's software designers who would be able to sell and produce Arabized products, not only to the local market but also to all other Arabic speaking countries. From a social perspective, expanding the use of specialized Arabic content software would allow for a greater margin of knowledge accessibility to the region with implications on the educational, creative, and human capital development. Such software would allow for the creation, cataloging, and organization of Arab-based content and knowledge. This, in turn, would allow countries in the Arab region, and most importantly Oman, to harness its own creative abilities for change and development.

Furthermore, in the near future, we will see how open source unlock the potential of a new generation of technologies—the Internet of Things (IoT), big data, and cloud computing—that would create multibillion dollars in value. Whether it is a web browser, a web server, or even a platform, FLOSS based technologies, and solutions have dominated the market share during the last few years. This dominance is expected to continue to grow in the future. Robustness, reliability, security, and performance are some of the reasons why websites and servers have been furnished with FLOSS solutions. Additionally, the world is witnessing a shift toward cloud computing and mobile devices. This future trend will boost the dominance of FLOSS, as it is leading the innovation in this domain.

FLOSS has proven to be an extremely valuable tool for accelerating research in various fields of IT and engineering in order to address the needs of society in the future. Many scholars use FLOSS platforms to conduct research in Cloud Computing (openstack.org), Big Data (Hadoop & Spark), and IoT (Kaa & Linux RTOS).

It is essential for preparing a roadmap for a sustainable deployment to examine different FLOSS experiences of other countries to draw lessons that will guide FLOSS deployment roadmap in Oman. While countries share the same interest in FLOSS benefits, every nation has its own culture and background that influence the approach of deploying FLOSS.

The USA, for instance, is considered as one of the pioneers in FLOSS growth and deployment. NASA is one of the organizations that recognized the benefits of adopting FLOSS, including increased software quality, reduced development costs, faster development cycles, and reduced barriers to public–private collaboration [1–3]. One can observe that FLOSS deployment at the USA was successful for three main reasons: Strong R&D contribution from academia and research units; Policies have been devised to help in the adoption of FLOSS at governmental organizations; a sustainable ecosystem was created with a well-defined demand and supply chain.

In contrast, France has established an e-government agency by the Prime Ministry. This agency has strongly recommended the implementation and encouragement of FLOSS and open standards. This has led to a wide deployment of FLOSS, mainly in the public sector. Currently, France is considered as the largest example of a public administration using open source on workstations [4, 5]. France's motivation behind FLOSS adoption was mainly to become independent from proprietary software and to achieve savings in software licensing costs.

Germany has started early with FLOSS initiatives and has been successful in both the deployment of FLOSS and the adoption of open standards. One of the benefits of this deployment was cost saving [6]. It is worth noting that there was a strong contribution from universities, research units, and the community toward the sustainability of FLOSS deployment.

On the other hand, Malaysia's success [7–12] is attributed to a number of reasons mainly, Establishment of FLOSS Center of Excellence, Launch of important Pilot Projects, Tripartite Collaboration towards FLOSS ecosystem, Creation of Critical Mass of FLOSS demand and supply, Assurance of real Transfer of Technology (ToT), Establishment of sustainable communities, Formulation of policies to facilitate the adoption of FLOSS, and Establishment of a "Knowledge Sharing Bank". The Iranian experience with FLOSS has targeted localization and a number of research studies have helped in FLOSS deployment in Iran [13].

Brazil [14, 15] has promoted FLOSS to ensure that citizens have the right to access public services regardless of the platform they wish to use. In addition, Brazil was able to save over $120 million per year by switching to FLOSS. Furthermore, the Brazilian government sought to create business initiatives and opportunities to bring technology to the poor. Therefore, Brazil success is attributed mainly to the provision of the policy, laws, sufficient funds, strong support, and R&D projects.

On the other hand, South Africa was one of the countries that faced a few challenges in the FLOSS deployment plan. In fact, the slow progress of South Africa in FLOSS deployment could be attributed to the following such as lack of adequate planning, lack of a realistic implementation strategy, lack of awareness, and lack of guidance and support.

It appeared from the analysis of the above experiences that sustainability and consistency of FLOSS deployment require securing funds to finance its projects and initiatives.

8.2   Status of FLOSS in Oman

To study the local status in Oman, two surveys have been developed. The first investigates the degree at which FLOSS solutions are being utilized in governmental organizations and prominent private organizations. We refer to this survey as the "User Demand Survey", or UDS. The second survey probes the readiness and willingness of the local Small & Medium Enterprises (SMEs) to develop and support FLOSS solutions. We refer to this survey as the "Development & Support Survey", or (DSS). This section presents a summary of these two surveys, how each survey was conducted, the process of handling responses, and some of the challenges faced while conducting them.

The adoption of FLOSS in Oman has been successful in both the public and private sectors. The ITA, for example, took a leading role in FLOSS capacity building by running short courses and workshops for training and certification. In addition, the ITA has developed the OeGAF initiative [16, 17] to (1) provide timely and secure access to essential information, (2) enable smooth integration of government services, and (3) improve the efficiency of service delivery. The initiative recommends the use of file formats that are publicly available. This is crucial to prevent vendor lock-in and to keep documents free of any particular technology or solution. On another front, the ITA has launched the G-Cloud [18], which is built using FLOSS solutions. Another program that was successfully launched by ITA is the SaS program for incubating ICT businesses.

Another example is the experience at Sultan Qaboos University (SQU). The university is using the FLOSS solution "Moodle" as a Learning Management System. Additionally, the curriculum of the Electrical & Computer Engineering program at the university includes many topics that deal with FLOSS philosophy and development.

In the public sector, the Ministry of Education has made outstanding breakthroughs in the curriculum by introducing FLOSS applications and development environments. Similarly, the Ministry of Health has built a comprehensive solution for healthcare facility management called Al-Shifa [19], which was developed using many FLOSS solutions. Furthermore, the Ministry of Commerce and Industry had launched the online service *Invest Easy* [20] using FLOSS solutions. Lastly, the Royal Oman Police is also using FLOSS solutions to develop 80% of its online services [21].

The use of FLOSS is not limited to the public sector only. In fact, many private companies use FLOSS, Rafed is one example [22].

8.2.1   User Demand Survey (UDS)

The goal of the UDS survey is to determine the extent of FLOSS usage, awareness, perception, and the potential for FLOSS adoption in the future. As a result, the survey responses would allow the team to answer the two following questions:

1. "How can organizations and educational institutions adopt FLOSS solutions?"
2. "What are the necessary measures to exploit the benefits of FLOSS solutions?"

The questions in the UDS survey are grouped into five categories:

 i. The first category tests the participants' knowledge of the FLOSS philosophy and benefits. The questions were designed in a way to explore how each participant perceives FLOSS, and whether he or she had any exposure to FLOSS solutions in the past.
 ii. The second category helps in understanding the requirements of these organizations in terms of their demand for software solutions. This category asks the participant to identify all software solutions (both FLOSS and PS) that are being used in the organization. Knowing which FLOSS solutions are used allows us to measure the current demand for developing FLOSS-customized solutions and the support for existing ones. On the other hand, knowing about PS solutions is useful in determining which application domains could be potentially replaced by FLOSS alternatives in the near future.
 iii. The third category of questions is concerned with the type of software licenses that are procured by the organizations. Some of the software licenses come in a package that includes installation of software, support and maintenance, and even training the employees on using the software. Other types of licenses include either software installation or support. Knowing the most commonly used type helps in making proper recommendations to SMEs when providing licensing packages to the target market.
   In addition, this category enquires about the allocated budget for purchasing software, and how that amount is split across installation charges, support, and training. Unfortunately, most of the participants opted not to answer this question. Therefore, the results are not reported.
 iv. The fourth category investigates how satisfied are these organizations with the software solutions that are currently used. Satisfaction is measured through inquiring about the reliability of the software, vulnerability to attacks, and lack of certain features that are deemed necessary by the participants.
 v. The fifth and last category attempts to measure the readiness and willingness of the participants to adopt FLOSS solutions in their respective organizations. The participants are queried about the challenges—that they think—are discouraging their respective organizations from adopting FLOSS solutions. Furthermore, the participants are asked to indicate if their colleagues are ready and willing to use FLOSS solutions.

The survey was conducted by approaching the participants directly through face-to-face interviews, by phone, or through online surveys.

The results of the UDS survey have pointed out that FLOSS solutions are mainly used by IT specialists at data centers (servers and database platforms), and rarely used on personal computers by non-IT individuals.

Figures 8.1 and 8.2 show interesting findings (among other results). Figure 8.1 shows that there is a huge reliance on software vendors in order to customize the solutions to meet the requirements of the organization. Migrating to FLOSS might minimize this reliance, leading to an overall reduction in software cost. Similarly, Fig. 8.2 shows that participants are lacking a few features (e.g., the ability to modify the code, better protection of data privacy, and more reliable software), which can be easily acquired when moving to FLOSS. Note that the choices made by the participants are predefined categories in the survey itself.

A large population of the surveyed organizations has reported low system performance and frequent software crashes in their computing systems. FLOSS alternatives can be offered to these organizations to improve the performance and increase the stability and reliability of their systems.

On the other hand, Fig. 8.3 reports the challenges associated with FLOSS adoption as reported by the participants. Accordingly, a few countermeasures need to be taken to overcome such challenges:

(1) More support in terms of capacity building and resources to encourage organizations to adopt FLOSS.
(2) A clear and succinct plan to migrate to FLOSS and integrate it into existing systems without disrupting the operations of the organization.
(3) Provide more specialized training to support FLOSS solutions.

Based to the reported size of IT staff in the participating organizations, training these individuals is manageable since the number is relatively small (approx. 80% of these organizations employ less than 50 IT support staff). In addition, the variation in the size of IT staff shows that the survey has targeted organizations with different IT support size, which means that the responses are representative of smaller and larger organizations. This could mean that the survey is actually a good representation of the demand in Oman.

Fig. 8.1 Types of technical support that the organization receives for software solutions. [105 Responses]

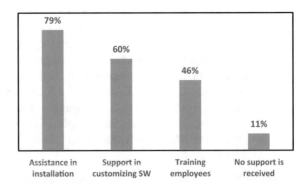

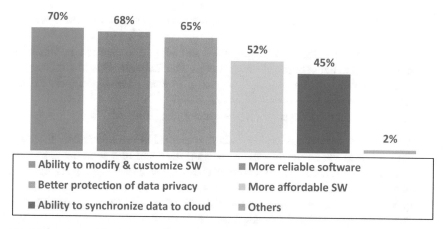

Fig. 8.2 Additional services that the participants would like to have in the software solutions that they use. [105 Responses]

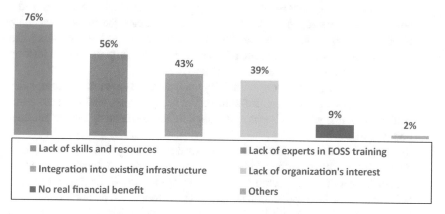

Fig. 8.3 Challenges associated with FLOSS adoption. [102 Responses]

8.2.2 Development and Support Survey (DSS)

The UDS survey measures the potential demand for FLOSS solutions. This demand must be adequately fulfilled with the proper supply. In this context, the FLOSS supply is represented by software development and customization, maintenance and support, and training. Without these components, it is unlikely that the FLOSS deployment would succeed.

The Development & Support Survey (DSS) was designed to measure the current supply of FLOSS solutions. In addition, the responses to the survey have provided us with an estimate of the future supply of FLOSS solutions. The results from the survey would allow us to identify the shortcomings in the current and future supply.

Therefore, the necessary measures can be devised in order to rectify these shortcomings.

The survey targets software development and support companies in Oman, as they constitute the main source of the "supply". The main question that this survey is trying to answer is *"Can software companies in Oman provide/support FLOSS solutions adequately and in a sustainable manner?"*

The questions in the DSS survey were structured as follows:

i. The first set of questions help in gathering general information about the company, such as the company's main specialization and how long has it been in business. In addition, this set enquires about the size of the company in terms of a total number of employees and the number of software developers. These questions help in understanding the capacity of the company and its ability to deliver adequate support whenever needed.

ii. The next set of questions asks the participant to identify all application domains that the company has provided and supported in the past. The questions require the participants to choose all the solutions—both FLOSS and PS—that the company has developed in the past. Answers to these questions would help in measuring the existing support for FLOSS solutions. At the same time, the responses will give a clear picture of where the FLOSS support is either lacking or insufficient for current and future demands.

iii. The third set of questions tries to identify the licensing types that the companies provide. This would confirm if the licensing schemes provided by these companies are in line with the licenses already adopted and used by the government and industry.

iv. The fourth set of questions enquires about the company's own experience in developing FLOSS solutions. More importantly, one specific question asks about the challenges that may prohibit the company from using FLOSS in developing solutions for various application domains. The responses to this set of questions help in recognizing the difficulties associated with FLOSS development, and therefore, paving the way for suggesting reasonable measures to overcome such hurdles.

v. The last question in the survey requests the participants to describe their business vision, plans, and growth strategy in the future. The answers are a vital indicator to whether or not these companies are considering FLOSS in their future plans.

From the data analysis, it is noted that most of the existing SMEs are specialized in software development and provision of services training and different types of support (Questions set ii). However, when it comes to the company's staff size most of them consist of less than 10 employees and most of SMEs have less than 5 software developers (Questions set me). It is vital to support these SMEs through initiatives that allow them to grow in size to be able to meet the market's demand. In addition, the results show that SMEs have good coverage of their support to application domains. This is important in order to fulfill a market that varies in its needs and requirements. However, initiatives need to be devised to encourage these enterprises to reduce their dependency on PS solutions and adopt FLOSS.

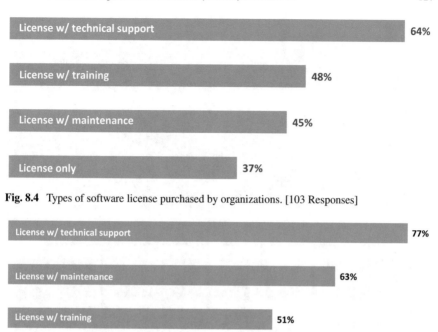

Fig. 8.4 Types of software license purchased by organizations. [103 Responses]

Fig. 8.5 Types of software offered by SMEs. [58 Responses]

In terms of licensing, one can detect the resemblance in trend when comparing Figs. 8.4 and 8.5. This means that the license schemes that SMEs provide are in line with what organizations acquire.

It is worth noting that the majority of surveyed enterprises have no previous experience with FLOSS development (only 28% of the respondents have developed FLOSS solutions). The results also revealed that business opportunities (70% of the responses), technical assistance, and human resources (42% of the responses) are the main challenges in adopting FLOSS for product development. To create business opportunities, there has to be a shift in the demand to lean toward FLOSS solutions. Similarly, and as discussed before, more initiatives and support need to be provided to SMEs to encourage them to expand their reliance on FLOSS.

8.3   Proposal for Sustainable FLOSS Deployment Roadmap

This section summarizes the main components of the sustainable FLOSS deployment roadmap in Oman for the next five years [23, 24]. The components of the roadmap resulted from (1) an extensive and comprehensive study of the interna-

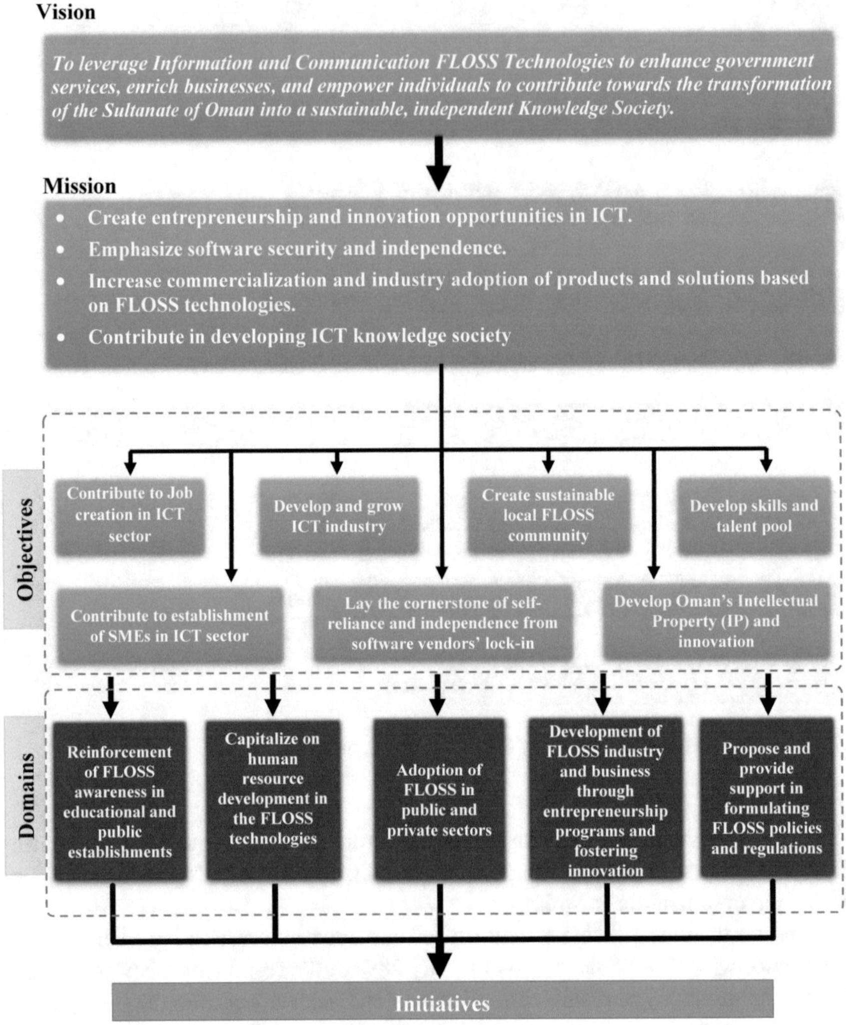

Vision

Fig. 8.6 FLOSS deployment roadmap framework for the next five years

tional experience, (2) the analysis of the local FLOSS status in Oman mined from the conducted surveys and interviews with different local ICT professionals, and (3) the exchange of views with external experts. This roadmap consists of a number of initiatives that resulted from the vision, mission, and objectives of the deployment plan. These initiatives were classified into a set of five strategic domains constrained by realistic timeframes (Refer to Fig. 8.6 for the 5-year FLOSS deployment roadmap framework).

In order to achieve the abovementioned objectives indicated in the figure, a governing body that sustains, drives, and monitors the implementation of the strategic domains needs to be established first. This body can be established under the name of *"FLOSS Center of Excellence (FLOSS-CoE)"*.

In addition, we have identified five strategic domains. These strategic domains constitute the basis of the FLOSS deployment roadmap for the coming five years.

These five domains are (refer to Fig. 8.6):

(1) Reinforcement of FLOSS awareness in educational and public establishments.
(2) Capitalize on human resource development in FLOSS technologies.
(3) Adoption of FLOSS in the public and private sectors.
(4) Development of FLOSS industry and business through entrepreneurship programs and fostering innovation.
(5) Propose and provide support in formulating FLOSS policies and regulations.

8.3.1   FLOSS Center of Excellence

A strategic direction toward a sustainable FLOSS deployment in the public organizations and private sector is to establish a FLOSS Center of Excellence (FLOSS-CoE). This center would serve as a national reference for leading, guiding, and assisting government organizations with deploying FLOSS solutions. In addition, the Center will undertake R&D; where it provides direction in the development and use of FLOSS through information, expertise, and physical infrastructure. Furthermore, it will facilitate collaboration among public sector, higher education providers, industry/business communities, and even play a leading role in the increase of human capital development in Oman. Our confidence in the success of FLOSS-CoE is stemming from the fact that many similar FLOSS centers of excellence were implemented successfully around the world.

The main objectives of FLOSS-CoE are

- Raise awareness on FLOSS importance in public and private sectors and the society.
- Promote and implement FLOSS solutions in the public and private sectors.
- Increase the usage of FLOSS in the public and private sectors.
- Formulate policies and guidelines.
- Develop educational/training materials and coordinate with concerned institutions.
- Support forming FLOSS communities in industries, government, and educational sector.
- Conduct and support R&D in FLOSS.
- Work on projects for the public and private sectors.
- Reduce the overall cost of software licensing.

The main goals of the various experiences of FLOSS-CoE implementations were to lead FLOSS initiatives, promote FLOSS, coordinate R&D, support community, and service business in general. Generally, the center of excellence is managed by a director or board of directors from a number of private and public organizations. Its scope varies widely according to the countries' visions and objectives.

8.3.2   COE Operation and Funding

As for its operation and funding, a number of models were adopted in the world. Some models opt for governmental operation and funding, through one or a consortium of few ministries. Some others opt for full control by the private sector.

However, in some cases, a combination of government and private sector may exist. In this case, a number of different combinations also exist. However, every adopted model is selected based on the local environment and objectives of FLOSS Plans for every country.

The establishment of FLOSS-CoE has many benefits to Oman, and therefore, the model to be adopted needs to respond to the requirements and the objectives of the 5-year plan initiative.

A non-exhaustive list of FLOSS-CoE benefits to Oman are

- Advance learning and innovation skills in ICT and national capacity building.
- Improve security and preserve sovereignty from both strategical and technological aspects.
- Increase technology operational support and customization.
- Improve market place competition.
- Reduce licensing costs.
- Reduce vendor lock-in.
- Improve knowledge of new ICT technologies and applications.
- Improve information access/social exchange with society.
- Contribute to improving the national impact on the worldwide community.
- Contribute to improving the leading role of the Sultanate of Oman in ICT.
- Contribute to strengthening the position of Oman regionally and globally.

A number of different models for the center of excellence were established worldwide. However, based on the study and the constraints in the local environment, it was recommended to establish a FLOSS-CoE to be funded fully (or partially) by the government (refer to Fig. 8.7 for the model structure). This model fits better the local environment and responds to sustainable roadmap requirements.

The suggested model will most likely succeed in its mission for the following reasons:

- It will endure less government bureaucracy and less business influence in operating CoE.
- It will have independent management to play an efficient role in achieving objectives.
- It will benefit and strengthen R&D in existing universities, colleges, and research units.
- It will be able to provide technical support in FLOSS for public and private sectors.
- It will facilitate the collaboration between public sector, academia and research units, and business communities.
- It will foster a local FLOSS Industry.
- It will support the creation and sustainability of FLOSS community.

Fig. 8.7 FLOSS-COE
funded by a number of
ministries

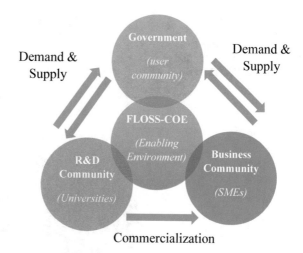

- It will assess the extent to which the objectives have been actually achieved (zero measurements will be performed when CoE is established; annual measurements will be performed and reported to the board).
- It will assure effective FLOSS Transfer of Technology (ToT).
- It will host management that includes diversified competencies to achieve FLOSS-CoE objectives.
- It will provide training, capacity building, and projects to bring up proficient people in FLOSS for development and support of products.
- It will reduce the overall license cost.

A proposed governance model for the FLOSS-CoE is presented in Fig. 8.8. In this case, CoE will be funded by a few ministries, as its scope and benefits cover many sectors that are distributed at different national levels. It is recommended to involve a number of ministries and the Supreme Council of Planning in its funding and governance. The ministries that are proposed to be involved are Ministry of Higher Education, Ministry of Education, Ministry of Manpower, Ministry of Transport and Telecommunications, and the Ministry of Finance.

The board of the FLOSS-CoE will consist of the main stakeholders of the FLOSS initiative, which might include members from:

- Government agencies (Information Technology Authority, Supreme Council of Planning, Tender board, State Audit Institution, Public Authority for Small and Medium Enterprise's Development)
- FLOSS industry (e.g., leading local ICT companies)
- Private sector (Banks, funds, venture capitalists, and financiers)
- Academic institutions (SQU, MoE, MoHE, and Other educational institutions)
- FLOSS communities (e.g., leading national and international FLOSS vocalists, proponents, developers, forums, experts, etc.).

The FLOSS-CoE board might be assigned the following tasks:

Fig. 8.8 FLOSS-CoE
suggested governance
model. Funding from few
Ministries (e.g., MHE, MoE
and MoMp, MoTC, MoCI,
SCP, MF, ...)

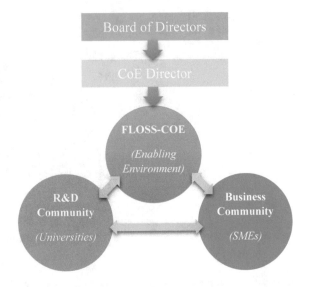

- Promote FLOSS industry and business opportunities.
- Approve policies, guidelines, legislation, governance, and standards.
- Publish recommendations and guidelines for the use of FLOSS and best practices.
- Provide advice on FLOSS deployment plans in a given agency and private sector.
- Support FLOSS in entrepreneurship and education programs through incentives.
- Provide coordination and collaboration management/leadership and orchestration by facilitating requests.
- Suggest FLOSS future research directors and strategic projects at national level.

The CoE staff tasks are (but not limited to the following):

- Create FLOSS awareness.
- Formulate policies and guidelines and facilitate FLOSS certification standards and programs.
- Conduct and coordinate FLOSS training for advanced and accelerated skills development.
- Maintain knowledge bank for sharing information and expertise.
- Provide technical support processes, systems/human resources, R&D, and testing facilities.
- Provide information, expertise, and physical infrastructure to support FLOSS deployment.
- Host the FLOSS portal in terms of news, report, case studies, forum for the FLOSS community, and projects.

Both the FLOSS board and the FLOSS staff will provide advice on FLOSS status, feedback, assurance of quality, record local obstacles, and publicize future direction of the initiative to the private sector, civil society, and government.

Given that the ultimate goal of the FLOSS initiative in Oman is to achieve self-reliance and sustainability of the FLOSS economy, the demand for FLOSS needs to be fulfilled. The public sector represents one of the major user communities in Oman. On the other hand, the private sector needs to engage with the FLOSS industry/business community that supplies FLOSS in order to accelerate FLOSS adoption. This initially requires the establishment of a number of communities; namely, the public/private sectors using FLOSS and industry/business community producing FLOSS solutions/services. FLOSS communities by means of smart partnership with private/public sectors can achieve self-reliance.

8.4   Conclusion

The sustainable deployment roadmap for the next five years, which is presented in this article, is a result of an extensive and comprehensive study of the international experience, the analysis of the local FLOSS status in Oman mined from the conducted surveys, and the interviews with different local ICT professionals.

This roadmap will lay the foundations for launching and developing the local FLOSS Industry. This evolving industry will contribute to attaining the major objectives of the government, which are centered on job creation, diversification of Oman economy to reduce the current dependency on oil and providing opportunities to increase the GDP per capita. This will also contribute toward building a sustainable knowledge-based economy and bridge digital divides in the Omani society.

The main remarks and findings of the study can be summarized in the following:

- The importance of FLOSS in many aspects, economical, business, security, self-reliance, and educational issues. A number of examples from around the world were presented to support this.
- The status of FLOSS in Oman, which was done for the very first time, will provide a relative basis to monitor the future deployment process of FLOSS in the Sultanate.
- Being the major driver for any FLOSS deployment initiative, a number of CoE models were presented. A realistic model is suggested for implementation in Oman.
- Five deployment domains were methodically identified with a number of initiatives to achieve the set objectives to be driven by the Center of Excellence.

References

1. Open Source Summit 2011, NASA, https://www.nasa.gov/open/source/
2. Open Source Software, NASA, https://code.nasa.gov/
3. GitHub, NASA, https://github.com/nasa

4. Open Standards and ITIL Lead to Open Source', France's Gendarmerie tells Korean ICT ministry, joinup, https://joinup.ec.europa.eu/community/osor/news/open-standards-and-itil-lead-open-source-frances-gendarmerie-tells-korean-ict-mi

5. French Gendarmerie, Open source desktop lowers TCO by 40%, joinup, https://joinup.ec.europa.eu/news/french-gendarmerie-open-sou

6. How Munich rejected Steve Ballmer and kicked Microsoft out of the city, Nick Heath, http://www.techrepublic.com/article/how-munich-rejected-steve-ballmer-and-kicked-microsoft-out-of-the-city/

7. K. Chamili, Y. Yah Jusoh, J.H. Yahaya, N. Che pa, Selection criteria for open source software adoption in Malaysia. Asian Trans. Basic Appl. Sci. **02**(02) (2012). ATBAS ISSN: 2221-4291

8. Malaysian Public Sector Open Source Software Initiative, Open Source Software (OSS)—Implementation Guidelines (2008), http://opensource.mampu.gov.my

9. Malaysian Public Sector Open Source Software Initiative, The Malaysian Government Interoperability Framework for OSS (MyGIFOSS) (2008), http://opensource.mampu.gov.my

10. Malaysian Public Sector Open Source Software Initiative, Web Application Guidelines (2008), http://opensource.mampu.gov.my

11. Malaysian Public Sector Open Source Software Initiative, OSS Reference Architecture (2008), http://opensource.mampu.gov.my

12. N. Binti Mohd Zahri, Open Source: ambitious, comprehensive transformation agenda: the Malaysian Public Sector OSS Initiative. Presented at the Free and Open Source (FOSC 2013) Conference, Sultan Qaboos University, Muscat, Sultanate of Oman, 18–19 Feb 2013

13. Xamin Server, http://xamin.ir/

14. E.E. Kim, F/OSS adoption in Brazil: the growth of a national strategy (2005), http://www.blueoxen.com/research/0000P/

15. M. Mannila, Free and Open Source software: approaches in Brazil and Argentina (2005), http://www.uta.fi/hyper/julkaisut/b/mannila-2005.pdf

16. Oman—Government Architecture Framework, Information technology authority, http://www.ita.gov.om/ITAPortal/Pages/Page.aspx?NID=559&PID=1848&LID=96

17. OeGAF, IRM structures and standards, information technology authority, http://www.ita.gov.om/ITAPortal/Data/ImgGallery/FID201111195657406/POSTER-3-IRM.pdfX

18. Oman Government Cloud (G-Cloud), Information technology authority, https://www.ita.gov.om/g-cloud/G-Cloud.aspx

19. Al-Shifa System Oman e-Government Services Portal, http://www.oman.om/wps/wcm/connect/2a19ffae-ade0-428b-9f7c-b30bdd874882/Al%2BShifa_MoH.pdf?MOD=AJPERES

20. Invest Easy, Invest Easy Portal, Ministry of Commerce & Industry, https://www.business.gov.om/wps/portal/ecr/about/faq/general

21. Private Communication, Wadee Al-Lawati, IT Projects Manage, Royal Oman Police

22. Rafed Group, http://rafedgroup.com/en/

23. H. Bourdoucen, M. Ould-Khaoua, A. Al Maashri, M. Sarrab, M. Amiri-Kordestani, Free and Open Source Software (FOSS) initiative: a proposal for deployment roadmap. A report submitted to the Information Technology Authority (ITA), Nov 2015

24. A. Al Maashri, H. Bourdoucen, M. Ould-Khaoua, M. Sarrab, M. Amiri-Kordestani, F. Al-Abri, H.F. Al Lawati, F. Al Saidi, K. Al Maawali, The long and inevitable road to FOSS deployment in Oman: opportunities, challenges, and caveats, in *3rd Free and Open Source Software Conference (FOSSC)*, 14–15 Feb 2017 (Invited Talk)

Chapter 9
Crowd-Based Methodology of Software Development in the Internet Era

Huaimin Wang, Gang Yin, Tao Wang and Yue Yu

Abstract In today's Internet era, software has infiltrated all aspects of people's lives, the trend of software-defined everything is essentially unstoppable. The classical methodologies in software engineering are expected to produce software at a low cost and with strong functionality by guiding the development process using industrialization methods and principles. However, as the complexity of software application scenarios and operating environments continues to increase, especially in the Internet era, prominent bottlenecks remain in improving the efficiency and quality of software development. Compared to the engineering methods, open source can attract tens of thousands of contributors to participate in the software creation process. This methodology is more deferential to each developer's individuality and aims to create a liberal, diverse, and democratic environment, thus stimulating the enthusiasm and creative inspiration of contributors on a large scale and ultimately generating greater collective wisdom. But the challenges in the diversification of individual interest concerns, the unevenness of contribution capabilities, and the unpredictable results of group collaboration make it unable to fully fulfill the tasks of clear and organized software manufacturing. In this chapter, we propose a crowd-based methodology that integrates the software creation process into the software manufacturing process, link a small-scale but well-organized core team with self-organized but large-scale crowd contributors, and transform a software opus to products in a timely fashion. Based on the crowd-based methodology , we design and implement the TRUSTIE environ-

H. Wang (✉) · G. Yin · T. Wang · Y. Yu
National Laboratory for Parallel and Distributed Processing, School of Computer,
National University of Defense Technology, Changsha, China
e-mail: hmwang@nudt.edu.cn

G. Yin
e-mail: yingang@nudt.edu.cn

T. Wang
e-mail: taowang2005@nudt.edu.cn

Y. Yu
e-mail: yuyue@nudt.edu.cn

ment to support the construction of software ecosystem. We illustrate the framework and key technologies and present typical application practices in both proprietary companies and online communities.

9.1 Introduction

—"I have a good business idea, but need a programmer to implement it!"

The hottest buzzword in information technology today is "software-defined", spanning from software-defined networking (SDN), software-defined storage (SDS), and software-defined data center (SDDC), which are part of a broader trend that people might call software-defined everything. Looking around the world, the total market capitalization of the top five Internet companies, i.e., Apple, Amazon, Microsoft, Google, and Facebook, has exceeded 3700 billion U.S. dollars[1] in 2018. *Mechanical Turk, AlphaGo*, and other breakthrough products have been invented by those companies, directly driving the innovation development of global technology. Software technology is widely combined with the urgent needs of traditional industries to create extremely innovative business services to facilitate our daily life. For example, when software meets the transportation, *Uber* is created; when it meets the catering industry, *Yelp* is created; when it can be embedded in tangible products, many smart hardware products are created, e.g., *Google Glass* and *iWatch*. It may be hard for people today to imagine how uncomfortable will be with no software support in their lives. Similar to the books that carry the text civilization using written language in the past, various kinds of software have become a new expression of information civilization in the Internet era.

Definitely, we do not expect that a consummate solution and methodology for software development can be found overnight. With respect to the development of computer hardware technology, until today, no software development methodology can promote software evolution at the same speed (i.e., the development of hardware capabilities is in line with the growth of Moore's Law [1, 2], while software technology cannot be guaranteed.

Case of ARM Ecosystem. The ARM ecosystem deeply integrates software with hardware. In contrast to Intel's ecosystem which has accumulated its own sophisticated software platforms, the main problem of the construction of ARM ecosystem is how to transform and optimize various kinds of open source and commercial software to be better compatible with the ARM hardware in a high efficiency and quality way, assisting the relating companies in the ARM community in delivering their products to the market rapidly. However, the transformation and optimization processes cover almost all software stacks, including the operating system, database, web applications, and the infrastructures for cloud computing and big data, which are beyond the capability of traditional methodologies in software engineering.

---

[1] https://www.statista.com/statistics/277483/market-value-of-the-largest-internet-companies-worldwide/.

To address the software challenges in the Internet age, we propose crowd-based software development methodology and its supporting environment called TRUSTIE. Our main idea is based on the linking viewpoint, i.e., effectively linking different types of development activities and different types of development collaborators to improve the innovation efficiency of the software ecosystem and reduce the cost, thereby optimizing the business patterns of all stakeholders. The remainder of this chapter is organized as follows: Sect. 9.2 introduces the methodology of TRUSTIE and the key concepts underlying the crowd-based software development methodology. Section 9.3 presents the framework and typical algorithms in TRUSTIE, as well as the related support platform and tools. Section 9.4 describes the application of TRUSTIE.

9.2   The TRUSTIE Methodology

In this section, we illustrate the classical methodology of software engineering, open source, and the main idea of crowd-based software development methodology.

9.2.1   Software Engineering and Software Manufacturing

The main question in software engineering is how to continuously improve the development efficiency and software quality. Since the 1960s, software practitioners have noted that strong challenges have arisen from the backward mode of software production. To address the "software crisis" [3], the concept of "software engineering" [4] was proposed. Practitioners aimed to implement systematic mechanisms to manage software developers and development activities in the form of a "project". This strategy is expected to produce software at a low cost and with strong functionality and high quality by guiding the software development process using industrialization methods and principles. In this concept, there is no essential difference between software development and industrial activities, e.g., automobile manufacturing, garment production, and building construction. Both of these broad fields are expected to achieve increased efficiency through strict and precise task decomposition and personnel organization.

Under the guidance of this classic concept of software engineering, the academic and industrial communities have conducted continuous exploration and research on various aspects, e.g., development methodology, project management, and software architecture. These communities have proposed a series of classic methodologies, e.g., the waterfall model [5], the constructive cost model (COCOMO) [6], and component-based software engineering (CBSE) [7]. The most representative and comprehensive methodology is exemplified in the software product lines [8], which can be summarized in the following three steps: (1) extracting the public structure and characteristics of specific fields or similar products through domain engineering induction; (2) organizing developers to write code and assemble modules by formulating detailed and strict production plans based on standardized reusable software assets and the software development life cycle; and (3) building a batch of software products that meet the needs of specific markets.

In brief, we summarize the software development processes organized by the industrialization solutions as **Software Manufacturing**, in which the outcome is the software product or production-ready software. These approaches are very effective in organizing software development activities with relatively clear and stable targets. Over the years, such approaches have directly supported the smooth advancement of a series of technology-intensive projects, e.g., projects in the aerospace and aviation fields.

However, as the complexity of software application scenarios and operating environments continues to increase, the challenge of "no silver bullet" [9] has become increasingly prominent. Especially in the Internet era, software stakeholders have changed from small-scale specific groups to large-scale, dynamic, and open Internet users, leading to the recognition that the software development process is no longer composed of activities with clear and stable targets. For example, in an open environment, the requirements of large-scale groups cannot be frozen, i.e., the demands of users are dynamic. Additionally, in a complex scenario, software testing cannot fully cover the restricted search space, i.e., the test target is not clear. The software workers who are struggling on the software production line have also not escaped the challenges encountered by Chaplin's character in the film *Modern Times*. Even though the overall labor importation and workload of the software workers are maximized, prominent bottlenecks remain in improving the efficiency and quality.

9.2.2 Open Source and Software Creation

During the period over which other engineering methods have struggled for prominence, OSS has achieved remarkable success after decades of vigorous development. From the early operating systems of BSD and Linux to today's smartphone operating systems (Android), application container engines (Docker), and deep learning frameworks (TensorFlow), many high-quality OSS has gained more market share than similar commercial software [10].

Excellent open-source projects can attract tens of thousands of developers to participate in their development, which represents strong productivity in industrial production. For example, the Linux kernel has more than 400,000 contributors [11], while the total number of employees of Microsoft's multinational technology company is only approximately 110,000. In the world of open source, the philosophy of democracy attracts different types of public contributors to continuously contribute to OSS projects that interest them. The efficient reputation propagation effect motivates top universities and scientific research institutions to release the latest scientific research results to society in a timely manner. Further, unlimited potential innovation has motivated more and more software companies [12, 13] to achieve high-speed growth through the model of open-source development accompanied by a service payment.

Relative to the standardized and strongly organized engineering methods, the open-source method is more deferential to each developer's individuality and aims to create a liberal, diverse, and democratic environment [14], thus stimulating the enthusiasm and creative inspiration of contributors on a large scale and ultimately generating greater collective wisdom [15]. We call the OSS development process **Software Creation**, which is very similar to the process of creating artwork. Therefore, we refer to the software artifacts created during the creative process as the software opus, which is akin to works of art. On the one hand, in the context of ambiguous open issues (e.g., the requirement elicitation for innovative software), some unexpected solutions or so-called "killer applications" can be generated from the software creation process because of the inspirations of individuals or the swarm intelligence of crowd. On the other hand, challenges in the diversification of individual interest concerns, the unevenness of contribution capabilities, and the unpredictable results of group collaboration make this process unable to fully fulfill the tasks of clear and organized software production.

9.2.3 Crowd-Based Methodology

In today's Internet era, software has infiltrated all aspects of people's lives, and the wave of *Software-Defined Everything* (SDE) is essentially unstoppable. The unremitting progress made in the areas of engineering methods and open-source methodologies has made people see the daylight of fundamentally breaking through the bottleneck faced by software development, as discussed in Brooks's "The Mythical Man-Month" in 1975. When we rethink all kinds of software development activities, the concepts of "software manufacturing" and "software creation" are thought-provoking. If we compare software development to automotive manufacturing, the engineering methodology represented by the software production activities is similar to the assembly line for Ford or Toyota automobiles. This process splits the phase of atomization of software development activities (e.g., in the waterfall model, the life cycle of software development is divided into six basic activities: planning, demand analysis, software design, programming, software testing, and operation and maintenance). Through advanced production and management processes (e.g., the organizational model of the company), software development has grown from a small, personal programming workshop (PROG workshop) to a large group that can support hundreds or even thousands of large-scale collaborations (software bloc).

However, operating software in a virtual space is not identical to other labor-intensive industrial products, e.g., automobiles. When the technical barriers to the underlying infrastructure (e.g., storage or CPU speed) are broken, the large-scale mass production and transmission costs of mature software products are almost zero (e.g., copying CDs or hard disks). Consequently, in the field of software development, the advantages of scalable replication, the most significant improvement in

Fig. 9.1 The crowd-based
methodology model

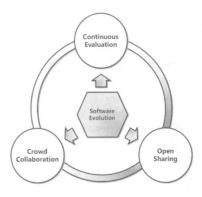

industrial production efficiency, have been greatly reduced. As the demand for new
software features continues to grow, the bottlenecks faced by software developers
are increasingly focused on software creation and the transition from creation to
production.

At this point, the high degree of decomposition of the development process and
the isolation in the collaboration of the development groups have not only failed to
improve the efficiency of software creation but also limited the scope of software
creation to a certain extent. In contrast, the open-source method, at the other end
of the scale, can fully create the atmosphere and environment needed for software
creation activities. For popular OSS, the development process seems to be similar to
global car enthusiasts participating in the design of a certain concept car, which is an
extremely effective strategy for innovation. However, open source has always been
organized by loose mechanisms, which has led to a large number of metaphorical
open-source concept cars unable to smoothly exit the software "Utopia" on time.

Building on the progress of previous innovators, we suggest that immediate reme-
dies to software development barriers can be found in the above two types of processes, i.e., software manufacturing and software creation. Currently, developers are
seeking an intermediate path between these two processes, e.g., the *Agile* development evolved gradually from the engineering method and the *DevOps* booming in the
open-source world. From our perspective, the new software development methodology should integrate the software creation process into the software manufacturing
process, and link a small-scale but well-organized core team with self-organized but
large-scale crowd contributors.

When the goals are not clear, the "core" coordinates the "crowd" to achieve creative work efficiently, and after the goal is finalized, the "core" organizes the "crowd"
to produce software products or transform a software opus to products in a timely
fashion. We call this method the **crowd-based methodology** of software development. The essence of this crowd-based methodology consists of three essential and
interconnected elements: crowd collaboration, open resource sharing, and continuous
evaluation, as shown in Fig. 9.1.

9.3   Key Technologies of Crowd-Based Methodology

In this section, we present the key technologies of crowd-based methodology in TRUSTIE, including crowd collaboration, open resource sharing, and continuous evaluation.

9.3.1   Crowd Collaboration

Crowd collaboration in an open-source ecosystem is based on the onion structure [16]. For a project team, such a structure consists of a small but strongly organized core team and a large scale but unorganized peripheral contributors. To keep the onion structure productive, various aspects are involved, including collaboration between developers, the connection of developers and development tasks, and the management of the development process. Figure 9.2 shows that multiple potential collaboration approaches exist among developers, such as @-mention and follow in GitHub. The developers can submit pull requests (PRs) or commits for collaboration between developers and development tasks. All of these approaches together promote collaboration in the deployment process.

Collaboration between developers. Many studies have proposed that social media tools can promote collaboration among developers, which is beneficial to software development. We used a mixed method, i.e., combining qualitative and quantitative analysis, to provide an in-depth understanding of how @-mention is used in GitHub issues and its role in assisting software development. Our statistical results indicate that @-mention attracts more participants and tends to be used to address more challenging issues. @-mention favors the solution of issues by enlarging the visibility of issues and facilitating developer collaboration. Our study also builds an @-network,

Fig. 9.2 Model of crowd collaboration in distributed software development

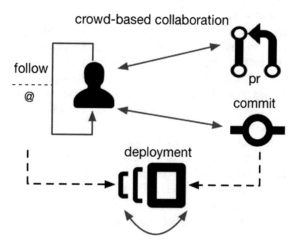

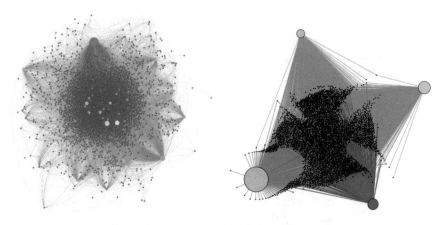

Fig. 9.3 @-network (left) and follow-network (right) in GitHub

as shown in Fig. 9.3 based on the @-mention database we extracted. Through the @-network, we investigate the evolution of the process over time and prove that we have the potential to mine the relationships and characteristics of developers by exploiting knowledge from the @-network.

The social coding paradigm has reshaped the distributed software development with surprising speed in recent years. GitHub, a remarkable social coding community, has attracted a huge number of developers in a short time. Various types of social network are formed based on social activities among developers. To determine why this new paradigm can achieve such great success in attracting external developers and how they are connected in such a massive community, we first compare the growth curves of projects and users in GitHub in three traditional OSS communities to explore the differences between their growth modes. We find explosive growth in the number of users in GitHub and introduce the diffusion of innovation theory to illustrate the intrinsic sociological basis of this phenomenon. Second, we construct follow-networks, as shown in Fig. 9.3, according to the follow behaviors among developers in GitHub. Finally, we present four typical social behavior patterns by mining follow-networks containing the independence pattern, group pattern, star pattern, and hub pattern. This study can provide several instructions for crowd collaboration to newcomers. Based on the typical behavior patterns, the community manager can design corresponding assistive tools for developers.

Connecting developers and tasks. The PR is the primary model for collaborative code contribution and aggregation between the core team and peripheral crowds in GitHub. To maintain the quality of software projects, PR review is an essential part of distributed software development. Assigning new PRs to appropriate reviewers makes the review process more effective, which can reduce the time between the submission of a PR and its actual review. However, the reviewer assignment is then organized manually in GitHub. To reduce this cost, we propose a reviewer recommender to predict highly relevant reviewers of incoming PRs. By combining information retrieval with social network analysis, our approach takes full advantage of the textual semantic of PRs and the social relations of developers. We implement an online system to show how the reviewer recommender helps project managers find potential reviewers from crowds. Our approach can reach a precision of 74% for top-1 recommendation and a recall of 71% for top-10 recommendations.

The continuous participation and contribution of the crowd are key factors for the success of open-source projects. However, given the massive number of competitors, it is difficult for a project to attract enough contributors by just passively waiting for enthusiasts to join in. Instead, the project should actively seek gifted developers. Most current studies have mainly focused on recommending experts inside a repository for some specific development tasks. To solve this problem, we propose the novel approach *ConRec* to recommend potential contributors across the entire open-source community for given projects. This approach leverages the developers' historical activities in projects to analyze their technical interests and technical connections with others. Thereafter, it combines a collaborative filtering algorithm with a text-matching algorithm to recommend proper developers. We conducted extensive experiments related to 5995 open-source projects and 2,938,620 developers in GitHub. The results show that the proposed algorithm can recommend contributors to open-source projects with the best performance of 63% in accuracy and solve the cold start problem as well.

Development process management. As an important approach in DevOps, continuous deployment aims to automate the delivery and deployment of a software product following any changes to its code. If properly implemented, continuous deployment, together with other automation steps implemented in the development process, can bring numerous benefits, including higher control and flexibility over release schedules, lower risks, fewer defects, and the easier onboarding of new developers. We conducted a mixed-method study to shed light on developers' experiences and expectations with continuous deployment workflows. Starting from a survey, we explore the motivations, specific workflows, needs, and barriers with continuous deployment. We find two prominent workflows based on the automated build features on Docker Hub or continuous integration services, with different trade-offs.

9.3.2 Open Resource Sharing

OSS community ecosystems (OCEs) can be seen as a complex network of resources from around the open-source community, including related open source projects, open source products, open source organizations, open-source developers, and users. OCEs have accumulated massive resources, and new resources are constantly being generated. These resources come in a variety of forms, including software artifacts (e.g., code snippets, and libraries), development documents (e.g., bug reports, design specifications), and behavioral data (e.g., review discussions, social communications). Open-source developers try to share these resources with the whole ecosystem as much as possible to obtain feedback (including criticism) and increase the

Fig. 9.4 Open resource-sharing pipeline

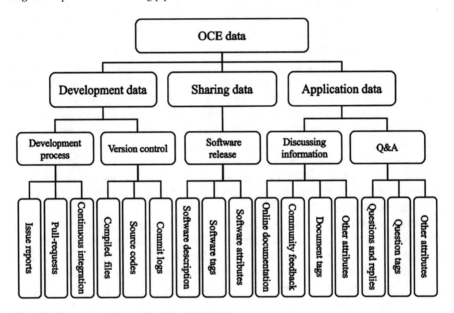

Fig. 9.5 Structure and types of collected OCE data

reuse rate of these resources. As shown in Fig. 9.4, to facilitate this process and fully explore the value of these resources, we propose an open resource-sharing pipeline consisting of three steps: open resource aggregation, open resource organization, and open resource reuse.

Open resource aggregation. As shown in Fig. 9.5, diverse resources such as software artifacts, historical process data, issue reports, and feature requests are produced and distributed dispersedly over various communities with the development of OCEs. To automatically and continuously aggregate such massive and diverse resources, we designed an aggregation system of high robustness, efficiency, and flexibility. The aggregation system consists of two processes: resource acquisition and resource bridging.

Resource acquisition. We use official APIs provided by open-source communities and web crawlers to obtain raw resources. Data crawling usually contains two interdependent processes, that is, crawling the raw web pages and extracting their attributes. However, direct extraction after crawling is not a suitable choice for rapidly changing and growing OCEs. To make the aggregation system acquire high quality and complete data, the system is designed with three stages: raw resource crawling, structured information extraction, and final data verification. These three stages are connected by the data flow and decoupled from the message queue and database. Their working state and interaction record are stored in case of exception or errors. Under this design, we can simply improve and restart any individual broken module without affecting and restarting other running modules.

Moreover, due to the various types of resources existing in OCEs, we make the aggregation system dynamically modifiable with external configuration files, which define the rules to generate initial page links, extraction templates, and verification specifications, among other possibilities. This approach provides a plugin-based feature to adapt to the resource diversity, and the only effort required to include a new type of resource is simply to write a new configure file; the source code remains unchanged. In summary, we have collected a broad variety of OCE resources of a wide range of types. The collected data currently cover nearly 20 well-known open-source sites, containing more than 14.2 million projects and 14.62 million posts.

Resource bridging. In spite of the diversity of OCE resources, open resources mainly exist in two types of communities: collaborative development communities (e.g., GitHub, Oschina) and knowledge-sharing communities (e.g., Stack Overflow, CSDN). The former resource type contains structured software artifacts, while the latter mostly contains textual posts. These two types of communities complement each other, and bridging them can expand the application value of OCE resources. While the bridging can be seen as a classification of posts to software projects, a conventional supervised ML-based classification algorithm cannot be applied due to the lack of training sets. Therefore, we use a text-matching method to solve this problem. We first extract the common attributes from different sources and define a uniform structure for each type of community. Two sets of resources are then integrated: posts and projects. Given a post, its title, tags, and content are matched with the name of a project, and each type of match is assigned a separate score. Finally, the match score between a post and a project is taken as the sum of these separate match scores with different weights.

Open resource organization. It is important to understand the collected resources before we can truly use them. An appropriate model and organization of open resources can lead to efficient and effective application.

Categorization-oriented organization. Categorization is considered to be an efficient way to manage information from large-scale data repositories. This approach clusters resources according to their topics and is quite useful for browsing and retrieving resources with similar functions. We propose a hierarchical repository of software features, which is an ideal technique to categorize software resources to support resource organization with flexible granularity. First, we extract a massive number of feature descriptions from online software profiles and mine their hidden semantic structure by a probabilistic topic model. Then, we present an improved agglomerative hierarchical clustering algorithm, seamlessly integrated with the topic model, to build the feature ontology.

Tagging is another popular and powerful mechanism for categorizing resources. To uncover the hidden semantics among tags, we attempt to induce an ontology-like taxonomy from tags. Specifically, we propose an agglomerative hierarchical clustering framework that relies only on how similar any two tags are. We enhance our framework by integrating it with a topic model to capture thematic correlations among tags. However, a severe problem for the current tagging systems in OCE is tag insufficiency. Consequently, we propose tag recommendation based on a semantic graph (TRG), a novel approach to discover and enrich tags of OSS. First, we propose a semantic graph to model the semantic correlations between tags and the words in software descriptions. Then, based on this graph, we design an effective algorithm to recommend tags for software.

Link-oriented organization. Although the two types of open-source communities emphasize different aspects of OCEs, they are highly correlated and mutually complementary because they overlap with each other by containing shared participants and issues. To mine the potential value in the two types of communities, it is necessary to reveal the associations between them and link them for knowledge sharing. For example, to explore hidden links between Android Issue Tracker and Stack Overflow, we focus on two factors: text similarity and temporal correlation. Intuitively, two related threads in different communities are more likely to have similar descriptions and discussion texts and arise in the same short period of time, which can be seen as a type of temporal locality. Based on this intuitive result, we propose an approach that combines semantic similarity with the temporal locality to link correlated threads across communities.

Moreover, social coding facilitates the sharing of ideas within and between projects in an OCE. Bug fixing and triaging, in particular, are aided by linking issues in one project to potentially related issues within it or in other projects in the ecosystem. We present a mixed-method study of the relationship between the practice of issue linking and issue resolution in the Rails OCE. Using a qualitative study of issue linking, we identify a discrete set of linking outcomes together with their coarse-grained effects on issue resolution. We use these findings to guide our quantitative modeling study of patterns in developer linking within and across projects, from a large-scale dataset of issues in Rails and its satellite projects. We find that Rails OCE developers tend to contribute most of their work within the ecosystem but that the distribution of the work across projects varies. Furthermore, using models of issue resolution latency, when controlled for various attributes, we find no evidence that linking across projects retards issue resolution.

Open resource reuse. Open-source resources are generated by the crowd; in turn, they serve the crowd and link the ecosystem. The most common way to reuse shared resources is by searching or recommendation.

Crowd-based search. Global open-source resources have become an Internet-scale repository that provides abundant resources for software reuse. However, how to locate the desired resource efficiently and accurately from such a large amount is a challenging problem. To solve this problem, we propose a prototype search engine that leverages the crowd wisdom to optimize the search result ranking. The number of times a software project was discussed by the crowd in various communities reflects its influence, and we treat the crowd discussions as an important ranking factor. For a user query that is formulated to find reusable software resources, we consider the semantic similarities between the query, the indexed resources and the crowd discussion popularity of the resources, and we compute a combined ranking score. Finally, we return the resources that obtain the highest combined ranking score.

Multifeature-based recommendation. Due to the transparency and openness of OCEs, a large number of external contributors are attracted to open-source development. The massive numbers of developers are driven by an interest in participating in specific development tasks. They have different personality traits, educational backgrounds, and expertise levels. Therefore, a personalized recommendation service may be helpful to reduce developers' time and effort in reusing proper and interesting projects. Therefore, we also propose an active recommendation approach to recommend resources for developers based on multidimensional features. We model the potential correlations between developers and open-source projects from three different dimensions: the popularity of projects, technical dependency among projects, and social association among developers. We aggregate the three dimensions of features with a linear combination and a learning-to-rank approach. Subsequently, the aggregated score is used to rank and recommend the top-K candidates.

9.3.3 Continuous Evaluation

The trustworthy software has attracted public attention in the area of software quality. Among the classic automation methods and engineering methods, software quality assurance is mainly achieved through formal verification and software testing. These methods have high costs and are mainly used for objective quality analysis. However, these methods ignore the subjective evaluation of contributors in crowd-based development activities, which presents challenges in adapting these methods to the continuous evaluation of software with changing requirements.

In an open-source ecosystem, a large amount of process data is produced through software development, which presents a large scale, diverse types, rapid growth, and rich content of big data. There are rich subjective feedbacks such as user requirements and evaluations. The process data, which form a complete chain of evidence from the requirement specification to the software code, constitute a new and important source of evidence for the analysis of software trustworthiness. Facing the new changes of an open-source ecosystem, we conduct evaluation works for projects, development tasks, developers, and issues.

Evaluation of resources. The amount of software in the open-source ecosystem is increasing more and more rapidly. Such a huge amount of OSS makes the rapid evaluation of software a necessary skill for developers. However, conventional methods have high costs and sometimes conflict with developer experience. We present a method to evaluate projects based on crowd feedback. To achieve this goal, we first combine all software information from different communities and then bridge them with posts from StackOverflow, which provides feedback regarding the software. In the process of connecting software production communities, we filter the duplicative projects, build a list of software and integrate all of their information. Then, we bridge software with posts from StackOverflow, and we link feedback with software by keywords and other descriptions. Finally, we evaluate the popularity of software by the number of linked posts, view count, and up-vote scores of these posts.

Evaluation of project. The integration and automation of the software development process have been key concerns in software engineering. We use large, historical data on process metrics and outcomes of GitHub projects to discern the effects of one specific innovation in process automation: continuous integration. We explore the impact of CI on software quality and the productivity of teams. We gather research metrics from three dimensions that are known to affect the rate of growth of projects' source base and the quality thereof: (a) the project attribute dimension (e.g., the project age, the project size, and whether the project uses CI), (b) the project popularity dimension (e.g., the number of forks and stars), and (c) the project development activity dimension (e.g., the numbers of opened issues and PRs and the numbers of merged and rejected PRs). By controlling for several known factors that affect the productivity and quality, we aim to discern the effects of CI. Then, we use multiple regression modeling to describe the relationship between a set of explanatory variables (predictors, e.g., usage of CI) and a response (outcome, e.g., number of bugs reported per unit time). Our findings clearly show the benefits of CI: more PRs get processed. Moreover, this increased productivity does not appear to be gained at the expense of quality.

Moreover, the open-source ecosystem presents extreme openness for developers to contribute, such as reporting issues. The extreme openness poses a severe challenge for the core team in project maintenance. Illustrated by the case of the issue tracker system (ITS), in large-scale projects, many undesirable and vague issue reports are submitted by external contributors (e.g., asking questions) because of their reluctance to spend adequate time to read and comprehend the contribution guidelines, which provide details on reporting an issue in a high-quality way and the type of issue that the project prefers to address. Thus, issue evaluation is a labor-intensive and time-consuming task for project managers. Furthermore, the core team members have to provide rapid responses and resolve the incoming issues in time to sustain the passion of external contributors. To help managers quickly evaluate whether the issue reports are a bug or not, we present a two-stage classifier framework to combine textual summary information and developer information that uses automatic classification techniques. The first stage extracts the probability of bug-prone and perplexity information of sentences for each issue from the free text, and in the second stage, some structured features about contributors who submit issue reports are provided, which can be expected to improve the performance of classification.

Evaluation of developers. Currently, more developers are adopting collaborative development models (e.g., pull-based model) in OCEs. The openness and convenience of such collaborative models reduce the contribution entries and promote developer enthusiasm. However, in a large OCE, the high volume of incoming contributions poses a severe challenge to project integrators who must review the contributions' quality. We first explore which factors affect the contribution evaluation latency in GitHub. We extract four indicators from the perspective of personal relations, namely, the submitter's success rate, whether the submitter is an integrator, the strength of social connection and the total number of GitHub developers following the submitter. Using regression modeling on sampled data, we find that these factors, including the submitter's track record, reputation, and social connection with project members, are highly significant. Contributions submitted by the core team members and contributors with more followers, more ties to project integrators, and higher previous PR success rates are associated with shorter evaluation latencies. In other words, open-source projects prefer a useful contribution from a well known and trusted contributor.

Furthermore, we aim to recommend appropriate reviewers to reduce the time between the submission of a contribution and its actual review. The two key concepts of our approach focus on the textual semantic of contributions and the social relations of contributors.

- The expertise of a reviewer can be learned from the reviewer's PR-commenting history. For a newly received PR, the developers who have commented on similar PRs frequently in the past are suitable candidates to review the new one.
- Common interests among developers can be measured by social relations between contributors and reviewers in historical PRs. Developers who share more common interests with the contributor are appropriate reviewers of that contributor's incoming PRs.

As a result, we first propose a novel approach to construct comment networks by mining historical comment traces. Based on the comment network and information retrieval technologies, we predict highly relevant reviewers for incoming PRs.

9.4 TRUSTIE Environment

Based on the crowd methodology and the key technologies, we designed and implemented TRUSTIE (**Trust**worthy software tools and **I**ntegration **E**nvironment) to support the modeling and construction of an open-source ecosystem. In this section, we give a brief instruction of the TRUSTIE architecture, and then present the typical support for ecosystem construction.

9.4.1 TRUSTIE Architecture

The core goal of TRUSTIE is to help form an open-source community ecosystem that connects diverse stakeholders to collaborate together in a community for continuous innovation and benefit. To this end, we built the TRUSTIE platform, which is composed of three levels: the data management infrastructure, the key technologies and mechanisms, and subsystems and services. The detailed architecture is shown in Fig. 9.6.

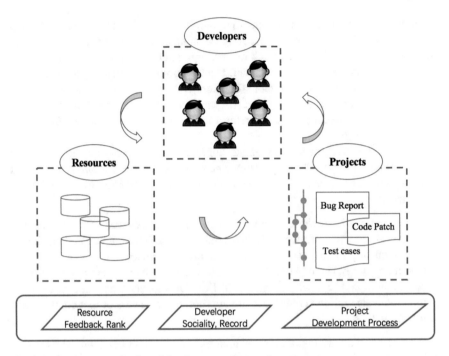

Fig. 9.6 Continuous evaluation of developers, projects and resources

Data management infrastructure: The construction and evolution of an open-source ecosystem is a data-driven process that also generates rich data. The data management infrastructure is in charge of data storage and providing a data access interface for upper levels. From the view of the source, there are mainly two types of data: the first is the data generated in the TRUSTIE community, such as project development data and user feedback, which are critical for guiding the construction and evolution of the OSS community ecosystem, and the second is the data collected from the Internet, such as the open-source application community and development community data, which provide reusable resources and empirical guidance.

Key technologies. The crowd-based methodology is the core and essence of TRUSTIE, which is supported by three groups of key technologies. *Crowd collaboration technologies* help extend the emphasis from only "professional-developer-centered" to "diverse-crowd-driven" and connect the small core team with large peripheral crowds for effective collaboration. *Open resource-sharing technologies* help transfer the "fragmented and disorderly" raw resources to "aggregated and ordered" ones and promote the effectiveness of resource sharing in and among teams. *Continuous evaluation technologies* transfer the traditional "static and single-dimension" analysis to the "dynamic and multidimensional" measure and evaluate the entities in the ecosystem continuously.

Systems and services. Driven by the key technologies, TRUSTIE was used to design and implement three subsystems that focus on various aspects of OCE construction and evolution. The *crowd-based learning platform* focuses on the professional development of developers in the ecosystem. This platform provides channels to introduce the incoming crowds and resources in the OSS community into a traditional classroom and to connect curriculum learning with standard project practices to help individuals develop their skills and prompt them to engage in OCE. The *open resource-sharing platform* collects and introduces Internet-scale external resources to the enclosed organizations and provides various channels such as resource retrieval and recommendation for effective resource sharing in and among teams. The *crowd-based collaborative development system* designs and embeds various mechanisms and services such as a development forum, process management, and code evaluation to connect the core team and peripheral crowds for software development.

9.4.2   Typical Support for Ecosystem Construction

The key factor for the construction and evolution of the OSS community ecosystem is "connection". The essence of crowd methodology is also "connection". This methodology emphasizes three types of connections and transformations: (1) connecting the peripheral crowds with the core team; (2) connecting crowd creation with business production activities; and (3) transforming the opuses created by crowds to the products managed by the core team. Figure 9.7 presents typical examples of the TRUSTIE support for such connections.

Connection between the core team and peripheral crowds: TRUSTIE incorporates various channels for connecting the core team and peripheral crowds. For example,

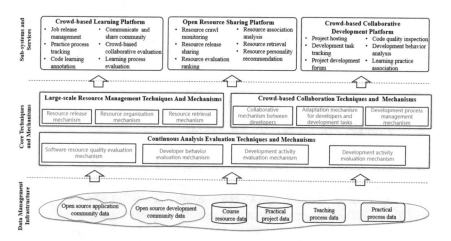

Fig. 9.7   TRUSTIE architecture

the discussion module is embedded in all three subsystems, which provides a convenient way for participants to communicate and form a micro-community. The task assignment mechanism connects them through tasks, and the resource-sharing mechanism connects them through resources.

Connection and transformation between creation and production: TRUSTIE opens both the project source code and the development process to the core team and peripheral crowds, providing corresponding mechanisms to connect the crowds' creation with business production. The crowds can express their requirements or comments (*innovation*) freely in TRUSTIE, and the core team can then be inspired to arrange corresponding tasks in the development plan (*task*). The crowds with necessary skills can also realize the innovations into source code (*innovation realization*) and submit the results to the core team, and the core team can merge the crowds' contributions into the product after reviews, or they can assign the task to the proper developer to implement (*task implementation*). The crowds can obtain and experience the product and share their feedback (*use and feedback*), and a large amount of feedback provides valuable evidence to rank and recommend reusable resources for software production.

Connection and transformation between opus and product: The outcome of crowd creation can be viewed as a type of *opus* that is inspiration-driven, and the outcome of business production is a type of *product* that is market-requirement-oriented. In the process of the connection and transformation between crowd creation and business production, opuses such as crowd innovation, code snippets, and feedback are connected and transformed into corresponding products such as development tasks, product code and reusable resources.

9.5 Application Scenarios

There have been many successful applications and practices based on crowd-based methodology, demonstrating the effectiveness of this approach. We briefly introduce two typical cases: practices in software companies and practices in online communities.

9.5.1 Practices in Software Companies

Neusoft is one of the leading IT solution and service providers in China. This company faces many challenges in increasing productivity due to its large volume of employees such as the reuse of company assets, cross-team collaboration, shortening of the development cycle, reduction of costs, and reduction of defect rates.

To consolidate the Neusoft production platform, we provide a new software development environment named TRUSTIE CDE that is based on the crowd-based methodology. This platform takes advantage of the mechanisms of the crowd method:

Table 9.1 Practical examination of the enhanced platform

	Exp. scale	Exp. domain	Reuse rate	Collaboration efficiency	Rate of defect reduce
Exp. 1	• 300 persons • 507 man months • 8 projects	Application software A: Health insurance B: Health information	↑70%	↑65%	↓31.5% for A ↓35.4% for B
Exp. 2	• 100 persons • 6 projects	Application software Tax	↑20%	↑45.69%	↓20%
Exp. 3	• 400 persons • 60 months	Application software Navigation	↑121 components in 11 categories	↑63.64%	↓18.7%
Exp. 4	• 261 persons • 6 projects • 12 months	Application software E-Government	326 software resources	↑41% for design ↑24.5% for coding	↓17.2% for requirement ↓17.8% for design ↓16.9% for coding
Exp. 5	• Millions of LOC in projects • 36 months	Infrastructure software Cloud computing	↑20%	↑30%	↓25%

the large-scale sharing of assets, cross-team collaboration, flexible production lines, and user feedback tracking. These mechanisms integrate collective wisdom to help the core teams in Neusoft make effective decisions. Several experiments have been conducted on more than 20 large software projects to examine the effect of the new platform. As shown in Table 9.1, we find that the crowd methodology can significantly improve the reuse rate, collaboration efficiency, and software quality in these projects.

9.5.2 Practices in Online Communities

Based on the crowd methodology, TRUSTIE fosters prosperous online communities centered around open sharing and collaborative development, as shown in Fig. 9.8. This framework has become a well-known software development and innovation ecosystem in China.

Currently, there are more than 3,900,000 projects and 14,200,000 posts in resource-sharing services, as shown in Fig. 9.9a. The data are collected from the most popular open-source communities and knowledge-sharing communities all over

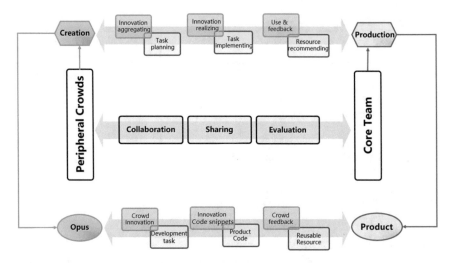

Fig. 9.8 Three types of connections and transformation in TRUSTIE

the world. TRUSTIE analyses and connects the large-scale data entities in different communities and then provides searching, evaluation and ranking services for OSS. Also, there are more than 52,000 users, 6800 repositories, and 2100 online software-engineering-related classes hosted in TRUSTIE. The typical user interface of a code repository is shown in Fig. 9.9(b).

9.6 Conclusion

In the Internet era, our daily lives have been redefined by software-driven technologies. Driven by massive decentralized crowds, OSS has achieved unprecedented success without strict centralized control. We study the core mechanisms behind the rapid development of OSS comprehensively and compare its development patterns with those of traditional software engineering approaches. We propose a crowd-based methodology to bridge the two paradigms of engineering and crowd wisdom methods, which enables crowd-oriented collaboration among internal development teams and external crowds by combining software innovation and software manufacturing.

The crowd-based methodology consists of three important components: crowd collaboration, open resource sharing, and continuous evaluation. Based on the crowd-based methodology, we built the TRUSTIE environment, which embeds multiple technologies and mechanisms to support the modeling and construction of the OSS community ecosystem. Over nearly ten years of evolution, TRUSTIE has enabled the formation of three typical and interconnected communities for crowd learning, open sharing, and collaborative development. The practices in software companies and

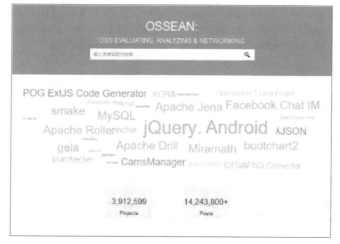

(a) Open sharing community

(b) Collaborative development community

Fig. 9.9 The online communities in TRUSTIE. **a** Open sharing community. **b** Collaborative development community

communities show that the crowd-based methodology and the TRUSTIE environment can strongly support ecosystem modeling and construction and bring substantial benefits to practical research institutions and business enterprises.

References

1. G.E. Moore, Cramming more components onto integrated circuits. IEEE Solid-State Circuits Soc. Newsl. **20.3**, 33–35 (2006). Reprinted from Electronics, vol. 38, no 8, pp. 114 ff, 19 Apr 1965
2. G.E. Moore, Cramming more components onto integrated circuits. Proc. IEEE **86**(1), 82–85 (1998)
3. P. Naur, R. Brian (eds.), Software engineering: Report on a conference sponsored by the NATO SCIENCE COMMITTEE, Garmisch, Germany, 7th to 11th October 1968. Nato (1969)
4. R.S. Pressman, *Software Engineering: A Practitioner's Approach* (Palgrave Macmillan, London, 2005)
5. W.W. Royce, Managing the development of large software systems: concepts and techniques, in *Proceedings of the 9th International Conference on Software Engineering* (IEEE Computer Society Press, 1987)
6. B.W. Boehm, *Software Engineering Economics*, vol. 197 (Prentice-Hall, Englewood Cliffs (NJ), 1981)
7. R. Niekamp, *Software Component Architecture* (Gestión de Congresos-CIMNE/Institute for Scientific Computing, TU Braunschweig, 2005)
8. P. Clements, N. Linda, *Software Product Lines* (Addison-Wesley, Boston, 2002)
9. F. Brooks, H.J. Kugler, *No Silver Bullet* (1987)
10. B.D. Software, N. Bridge, *Future of Open Source Survey Results* (2015)
11. M. Zhou, Q. Chen, A. Mockus, F. Wu, On the scalability of Linux kernel maintainers' work, in *Proceedings of the 2017 11th Joint Meeting on Foundations of Software Engineering and (ESEC/FSE 2017)* (ACM, New York, NY, USA, 2017), pp. 27–37
12. M. Zhou, A. Mockus, X. Ma, L. Zhang, H. Mei, Inflow and retention in OSS communities with commercial involvement: a case study of three hybrid projects. ACM Trans. Softw. Eng. Methodol. (TOSEM) **25**(2), 13 (2016)
13. E. Kalliamvakou, D. Damian, K. Blincoe et al., Open source-style collaborative development practices in commercial projects using GitHub, in *ICSE* (2015), pp. 574–585
14. D. Rushkoff, *Open Source Democracy: How Online Communication is Changing Offline Politics*, vol. 10753 (Demos, 2003)
15. J. Surowiecki, The wisdom of crowds: why the many are smarter than the few and how collective wisdom shapes business. *Economies, Societies and Nations* **296** (2004)
16. Y.W. Ye, K. Kishida, Toward an understanding of the motivation of open source software developers, in *Proceedings of 25th International Conference on Software Engineering* (2003), pp. 419–429

Printed in the United States
By Bookmasters